My Name is Not My Own

Kyra Coffie

I sincerely thank the librarians, archivists, curators, and staff who assisted me with my research. Your patience and knowledge were essential to helping me discover my ancestors.

Arlington Public Library
Daughters of the American Revolution
East Carolina University, Joyner Library
Halifax County Public Library
Library of Congress
Library of Virginia
Robeson County Public Library
Smithsonian's National Museum of African American History and Culture
University of North Carolina at Chapel Hill, Wilson Library
Virginia Museum of History & Culture

And to Ellen - you were right about everything. Thank you for your support and guidance.

Table of Contents

Our family hails from North Carolina and Virginia, specifically Robeson County in North Carolina and Halifax, Henry, Pittsylvania, Amherst, Nelson, Appomattox, Albemarle, and Lynchburg Counties in Virginia. Researching our family involves starting with the known (parents and grandparents) and venturing into the unknown (great-great-great grandparents, unidentified relatives, and enslavers). This endeavor is exciting, heartbreaking, tedious, and rewarding; it grounds us as individuals and also as a family.

Historical Records

There is an unfathomable amount of records to help genealogists recreate their family history. It can be overwhelming; you can look through thousands of records for one crucial clue, which leads to another clue, which in turn leads to the information you're seeking. In order to fully understand this book, you must understand the different types of historical records that genealogists use.

Our ancestors' lives were recorded personally as well as by local, state, and federal officials. The table below includes the records I've used to compile our family's history, along with their definitions.

Record	Definition	Category
Family Papers	Personal correspondence, Bibles, and ledgers, which were all frequently donated to museum and university libraries	Personal
Family Histories	Genealogies compiled by a family member	
Church Records	Births, baptisms, tithes, and burials	Local
Newspapers	Obituaries, land sales, and notable moments	
Chancery	Legal proceedings	State
Cohabitation Registers	The state's formal recognition of formerly enslaved people's relationships	
Colored Poll Books	Voting records for formerly enslaved people	
Land Grants/Deeds	Individual's or family's land holdings	
Ship Manifests	List of ship passengers	
State Census	This census occurs every ten years (years that end in "5")	
Vital Records	Birth, death, marriage, adoption, and divorce documents	
Tax Recods	Personal property and land tax records	
Wills/Probate Documents	Estate instructions, heirs, and inventory	
Federal Census	Counts the members of a household and includes race, sex, marital status, birthplace, and other vital statistics	Federal
Military Records/Pensions	Military records for service members	

These records can be found online, although I must admit that examining a 200-year-old document in person is pretty darn cool. Whatever can't be found online, genealogists can find in public, research, and university libraries, the Library of Congress, the National Archives, courthouses, churches, cemeteries, and museums. It can be a time-intensive and expensive task; some collections can only be seen in person, requiring researchers to travel to those locations. For example, I went to the Virginia Museum of History and Culture to examine records related to the Spraggins family. There are nearly 5000 items in the collection. It could have taken months to review the documents! Instead, I looked at the finding aid (akin to a table of contents) to find relevant documents by scanning for the names of the enslavers. I spent nearly two days at VMHC and scanned some pertinent documents to examine later. Cemeteries are another type of historical record that don't tend to move around, so I had to visit those in person as well. Our ancestors' final resting places range from New York down to North Carolina. I traveled over 3,000 miles, visited countless libraries, and operated more microfilm machines than I can remember to gather the information I needed to write this book.

Halifax County Will Book, 29, (1865-1869), Index Page

William Penick's (1799-1878) will
An example of the generational wealth white enslavers could pass to their descendants.

Finding The Records and Staying Organized

I began my research on Ancestry.com. Most amateur genealogists use this website to start their ancestral journey. Ancestry.com contains digitized records from over 80 countries. Despite containing 30 billion records, it's not always enough, but it's a good place to start.

Ancestry.com prompts you to enter information on yourself, your parents, and your grandparents, and then the magic happens. Little leaves or hints appear on these profiles; you can begin viewing public record files such as marriage certificates, census records, and other historical documents. A novice might accept all the hints, but this could inadvertently introduce the details of someone else with the same name into your tree. Ancestry.com's suggestion algorithm is pretty accurate, but I double-checked specific facts before adding them to my tree.

My tree grew to over 2,000 people, so you can see how easy it is to become disorganized and overwhelmed. I have an ancestry logbook where I record the last document I searched for, what I discovered, and my proposed next steps. I keep a grid and loose papers that help me track what sites and documents I've searched for or located for a family group. This is necessary because research isn't linear. I'd love to research a family, like the Smiths or Penicks, until I'm completely done, but that isn't possible or efficient.

Take microfilm records, for example. I can request microfilm from the Library of Virginia for the Appomattox County Land Tax Records from 1858–1864. While I have the microfilm, it's a better use of time to search for family surnames in Appomattox County during this six-year time span. I'd sort them into separate folders and then look at the whole lot later. Otherwise, I might mistakenly view the same records over and over. Microfilm can hold up to 800 pages, but they aren't always alphabetized, chronological, or indexed. Viewing microfilm can be tedious, as you must go page by page and read elegant but illegible cursive. I've learned to look for patterns like "cloud seals" or demarcations to see how the records have been organized. It makes it easier to scan a page without reading it.

Now that we've discussed microfilm and historical records, let's look at how records are created. Today, if we have a child, the hospital immediately records their birth, the child's parents, and other vital information. Back in the 1800s, notifications of significant life events weren't immediate or accurate, and if a child was born or a patriarch died, the event might not even be recorded until someone went to the courthouse to report it. If you know an event happened in 1858, you may have to look through the records for all of 1858 before you find what you're looking for. To avoid looking through records twice, you can see the wisdom of slowing down and looking for all your ancestors in a certain document before moving to the next document. Despite my best efforts, I may have overlooked a record. Though you may not believe it, I don't get upset about it. After all, during this journey, I'm sure there are records that were lost, nonexistent, or burned.

I intentionally mentioned records that have been burned to bring up my next topic: how do I know if a record has been burned? There is a phenomenon called "burned counties," which means the records in a certain county were burned (either accidentally or on purpose) before someone made copies. If a child was born, it was recorded with the county clerk. Those ledgers were copied and then sent to the state. That is why sometimes, if I couldn't find a record at the local level, I could check at the state level and vice versa. However, if the records burned before that duplication, they are lost forever. One such burned county is Appomattox County, VA. Appomattox County was created by combining four other counties in 1845, and the courthouse was burned in 1892. Some records can be compiled from other research sources, but some, such as wills, are lost.

When compiling records from other sites, here are my go-to sources:

Family Search

Daughters of the American Revolution

Archive Grid

State Vital Records

Find A Grave

Newspapers.com

Virginia Museum of History and Culture

Library of Congress

Genealogy Bank

Library of Virginia

Smithsonian National Museum of African American History & Culture

National Archives

DNA Painter

Someone searching in another part of the country would probably use different resources, but these were the most fruitful for my research.

Starting Point

I began tracing the lineage of my mother's parents, Lacy Garlington Smith, Jr (1923-1983) and Jean Mae Anderson (1934-1984). From there, I traced my family history, with some gaps, to the mid-1700s. Genealogy is detective work for ancestry, and just like Vera or Luther, you work with what you have and then go to secondary sources. I will take you along that journey so you can see the records for yourself, draw your conclusions, and decide if my research accurately reflects our family history.

Genealogical research is a treasure hunt without a map. This is why you always start with vital records, if you're lucky enough to have them; they're the crème de la creme of ancestry research. As seen with Lacy Garlington Smith, Jr, his birth certificate lists his father's name, mother's name, place of birth, and year of birth. This vital information allows a researcher to go back one more generation to discover that person's parents. This methodology works for those born after 1865. For those born earlier, you'll have to compile the information from multiple resources to match the information found in vital records.

Fastidious recording-keeping, especially for enslaved populations, wasn't the norm. Genealogy research can result in a range of dates of birth and death, inconsistent spellings, and unfamiliar abbreviations. You just have to roll with it!

STATE OF NORTH CAROLINA
NEW HANOVER COUNTY
REGISTER OF DEEDS
MORGHAN GETTY COLLINS

A search of our records reveal no trace of this birth

COUNTY OF_____, STATE OF NORTH CAROLINA   217

DELAYED CERTIFICATE OF BIRTH REGISTRATION

Name at birth Lacey G. Smith, Jr   Born March 2, 1923

Sex male Birthplace (city or town) Wilmington   County New Hanover

Attendant at birth Dr. Burnett   Address deceased

FATHER	MOTHER
Full name Lacey G. Smith, Sr	Full Maiden Name Barbare E. Melvin
Color negro Birth year 1895	Color negro Birth year 1893
Birthplace Robinson County, N.C.	Birthplace Hope Mill, N.C.

ABSTRACT OF EVIDENCE
Upon exhibition of an affidavit by Lacy G. Smith, Sr. father of Lacy G. Smith, Jr., certifying before a notary public under seal that he knows the birth date of this boy to be March 2, 1923, in Wilmington, N.C.; further affidavit of Dorothy Robinson, notary public of Pittsburgh, Pa. that she has examined the Smith Family Bible in which is written the birth date of Lacey G. Smith, Jr. as March 2, 1923 in Wilmington, N.C., I hereby commend that this record of birth be established as per amended V.S. Act 1951

I certify that the evidence described in the above abstract was examined by me or by my agent; and that, to the best of my knowledge and belief, such evidence complies with the requirements of the North Carolina State Board of Health for the delayed registration of births.

Date Oct. 23, 1951   P L Black
                           Register of Deeds

I certify that a search has revealed no prior birth certificate in the Bureau of Vital Statistics for the above named person.
          OCT 25 1951
Date filed_____   C P Sirick
                           Director Bureau of Vital Statistics

I HEREBY CERTIFY THAT THIS IS A TRUE AND ACCURATE COPY WHICH APPEARS ON RECORD IN THE OFFICE OF REGISTER OF DEEDS, NEW HANOVER COUNTY, N.C. IN BOOK 68 PAGE 217. WITNESS MY HAND AND SEAL THIS 20th OF MAY, 2024.

MORGHAN GETTY COLLINS, REGISTER OF DEEDS

BY: Theresa Davis
ASSISTANT/DEPUTY REGISTER OF DEEDS

If you are a history buff, you may recognize 1865 as the end of the Civil War. 1865 also marks the year when African-American people were recognized as United States citizens for the first time and when their lives were documented rigorously and systematically. For example, African Americans appear in Colored Voting Poll Books, the 1870 census, contracts, and employment records. The Freedmen's Bureau was instrumental in recording the marriage details of the formerly enslaved, because as chattel, "...they were in a state of bondage, they could not enter into any legally enforceable civil contracts" (Goring). Entering a marriage or a contubernal relationship required the permission of their enslaver.

1867 Freedmen contract
Courtesy of Library of Virginia

An early example of black people exercising their right to vote. After the 1877 withdrawal of Federal troops from former Confederate states, whites systematically disenfranchised black voters until the Voting Rights Act of 1965.

1867 Colored Voting Poll Book, Pittsylvania County, VA, District 5

House resolution establishing the Freedmen's Bureau
Courtesy of Library of Virginia

1870 population census, Lynchburg, VA

Clearly, 1865 marks a watershed moment for every African American's family tree. Before 1865, African Americans were treated as property; after 1865, they were included in records as full citizens. As property, enslaved people were routinely counted collectively, with reference to age and gender but not by name. For genealogists, it is frustrating and dehumanizing to determine which record belongs to which enslaved person. However, there are ways to complete this picture. As we did with vital records, we work backward.

Enslaved Billy's permission slip to marry a woman on Thomas L. Spraggins' plantation
Courtesy of Virginia Museum of History & Culture (Mss1 Sp716a)

1860 Slave Schedule, Appomatox County, VA

I will begin with the 1870 census, as this is the first census in which African-American people appear as individuals and family units. The census shows where they lived, who they lived with, and their approximate ages. This allows me to expand family trees to include aunts, uncles, and cousins, and it helps confirm guesses about the family. Where our ancestors lived is the most crucial detail. I make two assumptions about their location: they didn't travel far from where they were at the end of slavery in 1865, and they assumed the last name of their previous enslaver. For example, Mat and Kitty Hairston lived in Henry County, VA, according to the 1870 census. Months later, I found an 1866 Cohabitation Register showing Mat and Kitty Hairston from Henry County, VA, with the last name of their last enslaver, Marshall Hairston. Therefore, I knew my assumptions about location and surname were correct.

As we've seen, 1865 is an important date for genealogical records. Still, a genealogist must research a person's African-American ancestry as well as that of the enslaver. Slave codes forbade the enslaved from learning to read or write, and any mention of African-American people before 1865 is from an enslaver, their contemporaries' perspectives, or narratives recorded after the end of slavery. Therefore, the next step in the genealogical journey is to review the 1870 census where our ancestors appear, catalog the surname and location of those ancestors, and then input that information into a new record catalog to search for the enslavers.

The News and Advance, Lynchburg, VA, Dec 13, 1910
Courtesy of Newspapers.com

Newspapers can help fill out a family tree when missing census and vital records leaves a hole. Take this description of James Waller's death.

But first, a bit about the federal census. There is a government-mandated census that occurs every ten years and lists the members of a household. The United States has censuses dating back to the 1700s, and most are available at the National Archives (except for the 1890 census that burned in a fire in 1921). The census forms have changed over the years, and there have been schedules or attachments for different types of information. Some of the schedules were related to property or agriculture. For example, in 1850 and 1860, there were slave schedules. These schedules listed slave owners and the age and gender of their slaves. While abhorrent for modern times, these schedules are a valuable research tool. The surname and location recorded in the 1870 census allowed me to find the enslavers of some of my ancestors.

There are few documents that explicitly state which enslaver enslaved which person. However, knowing an enslaver's name allows you to build their tree (even if they aren't related to your ancestors), track their land holdings, read their family correspondence, visit their antebellum homes, scour cemeteries, pore over maps, dissect wills and deeds, and look for any hint or mention of an enslaved ancestor. It is a monumental task that reaps dividends, because you can find the lands of our ancestors, learn about their lives, and reflect on how far we've come since our enslaved beginnings.

Slavery

Before we delve into the lineage of my ancestors, I want to set the scene of slavery. This summation is primarily drawn from the Smithsonian's National Museum of African American History and Culture (NMAAHC). I strongly encourage you to visit NMAAHC, because it "… is the only national museum devoted exclusively to the documentation of African American life, history, and culture." African-American history stretches to before the 15th century (the start of NMAAHC's exhibit), and explaining every facet of that narrative would be daunting. However, knowing some of the context will help you envision the period before our ancestors appeared in the historical records.

If you've read the story of Joseph in the Bible, you are familiar with the concept of slavery and how a person could overcome it. This chart from the Smithsonian shows how slavery has changed since the 1400s.

While the attitudes of slavery were changing, Europeans began forming nation-states from what were previously disparate communities or kingdoms. England, France, the Netherlands, and Portugal emerged from these consolidations as the four major empires that exploited and profited from "…the forced migration of 12 million African people." Initially, Europeans and West Africans primarily traded goods, such as gold, ivory, spices, and sometimes enslaved people. However, Christopher Columbus' 1492 voyage to the Americas and the subsequent colonization of those new lands shifted trade from material exports to human chattel. (AncestryDNA testing from our family members shows that most of our ancestors came from Western Africa).

The World in 1400s	The World After 1400s
Slavery was everywhere.	Europeans refused to enslave fellow Christian Europeans.
The trade in gold, salt, and spices far exceeded the trade in slaves.	Enslaved people were dehumanized. Considered property, they could be used up and replaced.
Slavery was not based on perceptions of race.	Slavery became racialized.
Slavery was a temporary status.	Slavery was for life - a legacy passed down through the generations.

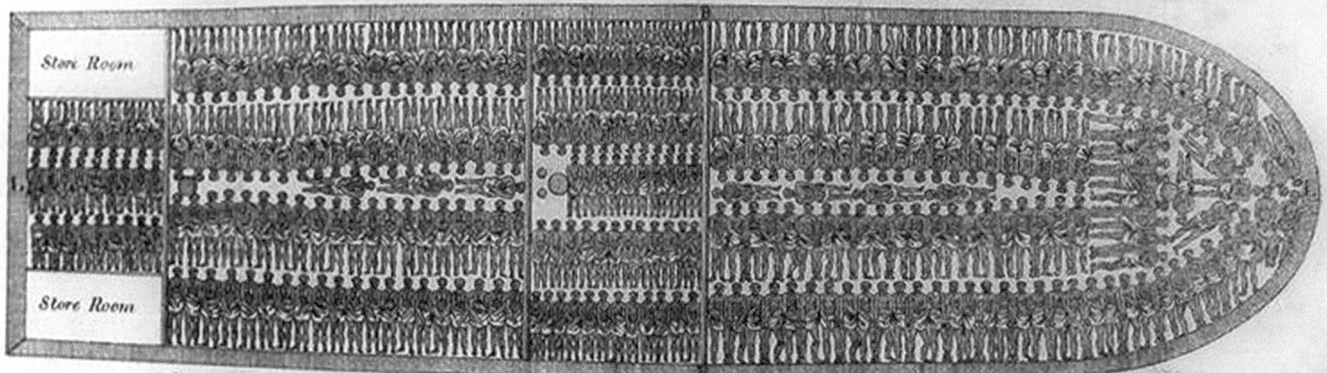

PLAN OF LOWER DECK WITH THE STOWAGE OF 292 SLAVES
130 OF THESE BEING STOWED UNDER THE SHELVES AS SHEWN IN FIGURE D & FIGURE 5.

Store Room

Fig 2

Store Room

Courtesy of Library of Congress, 98504459

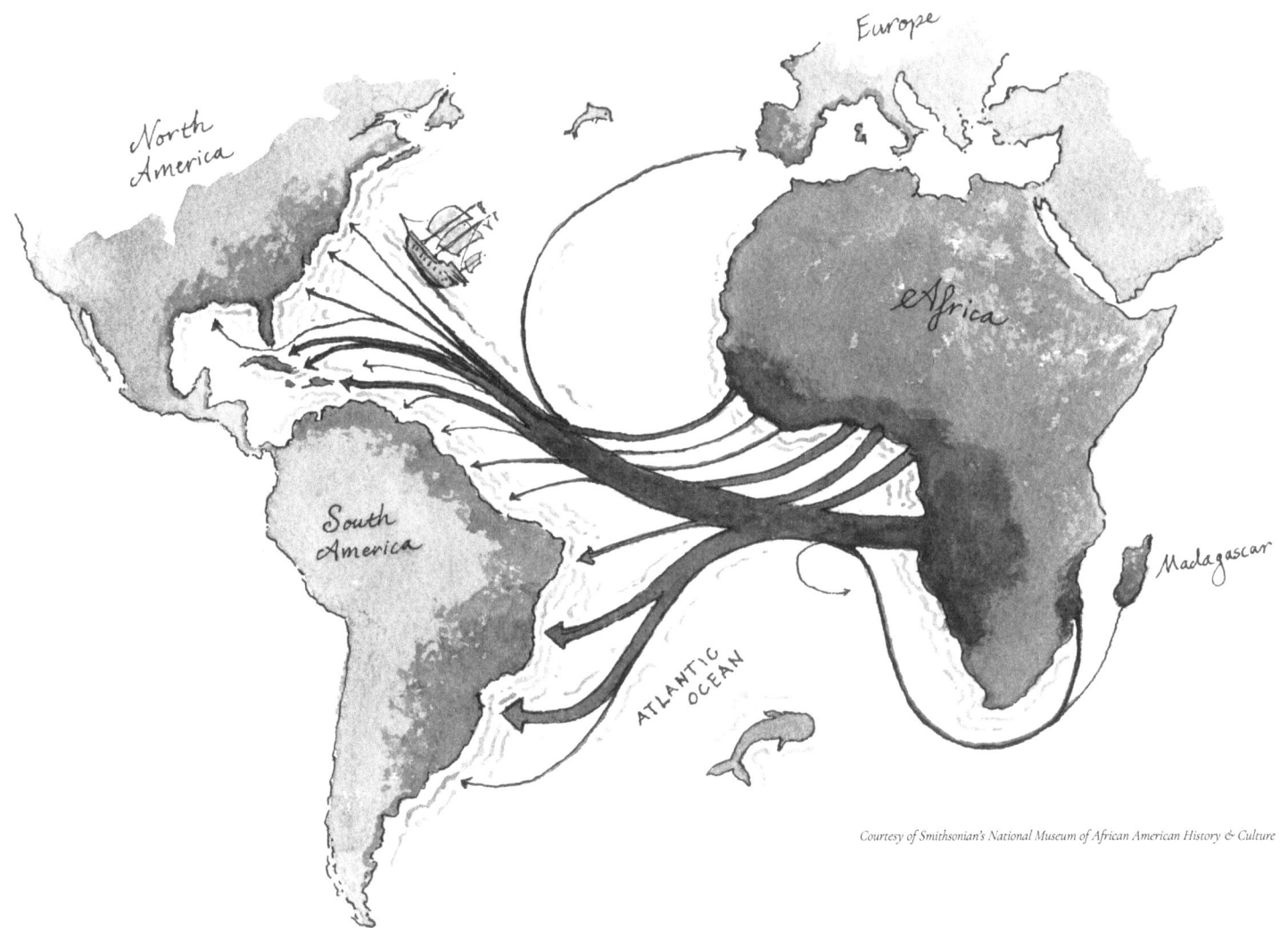

Courtesy of Smithsonian's National Museum of African American History & Culture

Colonization and the plantation system required enormous amounts of labor, and enslaved Africans filled that niche. To fill slave traders' ships, African men, women, and children were kidnapped, imprisoned in barracoons, branded, and transferred to slave ships. The slave ships traveled up and down the coast of western Africa to ensure their holds were full before journeying across the Atlantic. Slaves were chained together, laying in their excrement; some couldn't sit or stand, the women were raped, and everyone risked disease. Once in the Americas, enslavers visited numerous ports to find the best prices for their cargo while prolonging the suffering of the Africans. The slave ports extended from Southeast Brazil in South America to New England in North America.

Along the Caribbean ports, enslaved Africans were instrumental in feeding Europe's demand for sugar. Before sugar, honey had been the sweetener of choice, since sugar could only be grown in certain tropical climates. The brutal conditions and shortened lifespan of enslaved people did not deter the slave traders because the supply of slaves seemed inexhaustible. Farmers shifted from growing fruits and vegetables for personal consumption to growing more lucrative crops, such as cotton and tobacco, to trade and make money. Other cash crops requiring enormous amounts of enslaved labor were tobacco, indigo, rice, and cotton.

African slaves were sold on auction blocks, which often fractured families, and they began lives of servitude that typically terminated with death or self-liberation. The American slave trade included cities along the Eastern seaboard and major slave-trading hubs such as Montgomery, AL; Richmond, VA; and Savannah, GA. The experiences of enslaved Africans depended on their location. A Southern slave might prepare land for cultivation by clearing forests and transforming swamps while enduring crushing heat, humidity, and pestilence, while Northern slaves cleared land for cities and worked on docks and in mining quarries. The White House, the United States Capitol, and the Smithsonian Castle were all built using enslaved labor.

1844 Slave Manifest

From 1619, when the first slaves arrived in North America, until 1808, when the United States abolished the international slave trade (though domestic slave trade was still legal after 1808), approximately 470,000 slaves were brought to America. The number of slaves, through new arrivals from Africa and births to enslaved people already in the United States, had ballooned to four million by the Civil War. This period witnessed slave rebellions, the Revolutionary War, the Constitution, and the Declaration of Independence that says "... all men are created equal.." and yet excluded women, Native Americans, African Americans, and enslaved people. After the end of the Revolutionary War in 1783, there was an increase in the number of Free Blacks within American society. Paths to freedom included self-liberation, military service, birth, or manumission. Even so, these freemen did not enjoy the same freedoms of white society. (I haven't found evidence that our ancestors were free before the end of the Civil War.) Certain laws, such as requiring paperwork proving they were free or prohibiting the purchase of property, were passed that imbued superiority to whites over enslaved Africans, and these prejudices have continued, whether subtly or overtly.

This summary covering the 15th century to the 19th century is a sprint that doesn't adequately explain the hardships enslaved Africans endured. I implore you to explore our African-American history through movies and books, a visit to the Smithsonian's National Museum of African-American History and Culture, or online exhibitions at your local library or museum. Each enslaved person's experience is unique, because life was different whether you were on a sugar plantation, a cotton plantation, or a tobacco plantation. Combined with the temperament of the slave owners and their overseers, it is nearly impossible to describe the plight of all enslaved people. I've included this section to give you context on the time and place.

I've intentionally saved one part of this narrative for last because I want to leave a positive impression. Even after kidnapping, rape, humiliation, and family separation, people of African descent have proven to be strong, resilient, and proud people. Africans were not a monolith and had distinct faiths, cultures, cuisines, languages, and community identities. We, as African Americans, have endured what no humans should, and yet we have risen. We are entrepreneurs, mathematicians, seamstresses, craftspeople, midwives, and underground railroad conductors. As you continue reading, I hope you see the strength of these survivors. Under a cruel system, they lived, loved, married, had children—despite the ever-present fear of their children being sold—and set a foundation for us, their descendants, to achieve greatness.

Surnames

Family trees can get quite complex as you go back in time. After all, each set of parents means you need to do double the research. Starting with Jean Mae Anderson and Lacy Garlington Smith, Jr, there are 32 separate family lines that need to be researched. And as I've mentioned before, the extant historical records determine the success you'll have researching each of these lines.

Using personal, local, state and federal records I was able to trace the family of Jean Mae Anderson and Lacy Garlington Smith Jr. to the early 1800s and found 20 surnames. On Jean Mae Anderson's side, we have the maternal surnames Anderson, Flood, Harris, Nicholas, Powell, Randolph, and Waller and paternal surnames Fontaine, Fultz, Hubbard, Penick, Shipp, Spraggins, and Wade. For Lacy Garlington Smith Jr, his paternal surnames are Boswell, Currie, Hairston, Shaw, and Smith. (His maternal surname is Melvin, but I am not researching his mother's line.)

Of these names, this research will focus on the enslavers' surnames of Flood, Harris, Nicholas, Powell, Fontaine, Penick, Shipp, Spraggins, Hairston, and Smith.

I did not research all the names, because sometimes there weren't enough historical records to create a one-to-one connection with our ancestors. And as much as I love research, I don't relish building a tree for someone not connected to my ancestry. Sometimes I need to make some hard choices.

For example, take the surname "Boswell." Charlotte Boswell's marriage certificate states she was born around 1857 in Pittsylvania County, VA, before the end of slavery. The marriage certificate states her mother's name as Aggie Boswell. We can infer that there were Boswells in Pittsylvania County, VA. However, in the 1860 Slave Schedule, there aren't any Boswell slave owners in Pittsylvania County. While the 1860 census

shows ten Boswells living in Pittsylvania County, their exclusion from the 1860 Slave Schedule means these aren't the same Boswells who may have enslaved people. It's possible the Boswell enslavers didn't live in Pittsylvania County, or perhaps the census and slave schedule include different names or use initials for the same person. Whatever the reason may be, there are too many unknowns for me to comfortably add to my tree.

There are two details about some missing records you should know. First, the 1890 census is missing because it was destroyed in a 1921 fire. Also, the state of Virginia decided to stop creating vital records from 1897–1911.

These two factors make it difficult to track an ancestor's movements. Through deductive reasoning, I can estimate when a person was born, died, or married—for example, census records list whether a person was a widow or widower. Other than a walk through a cemetery or finding a family Bible, some facts just can't be known. Another category of missing records are those that haven't been found yet. Government buildings across the country contain hundreds of years' worth of records, and not all have been digitized. Compounding this challenge is the misfiling or misplacement of documents that no one can find. Until they are found and digitized, they may as well be lost.

I also want to address the rise of DNA testing and how I use it. I find DNA testing helpful, and I use it adjacent to my genealogical research, but I don't rely solely on it. I verify everything I add to my tree from multiple sources and treat DNA as a secondary source. DNA testing can also be helpful to expand a family tree, but I independently verify the results with other primary sources. (The Smith surname is a case study for combining DNA and genealogy.)

For some surnames, you will see an illustration that lists the production of their plantations. These numbers can be difficult to process because visits to the grocery store today involve grocery carts full of 1-pound containers of butter, 5-pound bags of flour, and 2-pound packages of meat. In our modern society, we're removed from the backroom processes that give us most products on store shelves. It is helpful to remember that during slavery, most of these items were produced by our enslaved ancestors. Creating butter meant milking cows—sometimes up to three times a day, separating the milk from the cream, and then creaming the milk until it turned into butter.

One cow generates between 7-8 gallons of milk per day and it takes 21 gallons to make 1 pound of butter.

Wool came from shearing sheep on the farm, and feeding the livestock involved growing large amounts of hay and many acres of grazing land. Take a moment to take in the plantation statistics at the beginning of each section below, because every item was cultivated using enslaved labor. To help visualize the size of the plantations, a football field is about 1.32 acres.

Finally, this book isn't intended to be a definitive look at our family. You won't find trees listing every marriage, birth, and death. Instead, I will explain my methodology and share interesting tidbits and conclusions I've drawn throughout this process. When reading this book, you can skip to the most relevant section that aligns with your interests. I find it all exciting, but I understand if you only want to read your family's lineage. There are also sections of the tree that are more complete than others due to input from a living heir. There are things we just can't know without help from living descendants; any skimpy branches are not an oversight but merely an opportunity for further research (with the reader's help!).

Enslaver Surname:	Location:
Flood/Anderson	*Appomattox County, VA*

ETYMOLOGY OF "FLOOD"

English: topographic name from Middle English FLOD or FLUD(E) (stream) or for someone who lived beside such a feature.

FLOOD PLANTATION STATISTICS

Wool 140 lbs

Butter 400 lbs

70 Swine

Wheat 1450 bushels

Peas/Beans 10 bushels

Oats 1400 bushels

Sweet potatoes 75 bushels

15 Cows

49 Sheep

Hay 12 tons

Potatoes 50 bushels

Corn 1375 bushels

Tobacco 9000 lbs

IMPROVED LAND 1800 ACRES

Bees 30 lbs

UNIMPROVED LAND 1426 ACRES

Successfully tracing Jean Mae Anderson's (my grandmother) ancestry to her maternal great-grandfather Warwick Garrett Anderson involved a marriage register (the precursor to marriage certificates) and a death certificate listing Louisa Flood and Charles Anderson as Warwick's parents.

I could not trace the Anderson line further, but Louisa Flood was a thread I could unravel. Louisa Flood and Charles Anderson had three children, and I researched one of those children, Rebecca Anderson. The 1910 census recorded Rebecca residing in Newark, NJ, and being married to George Eastman. In that census, Rebecca's mother, Louisa, is listed as living with her, which helped me find Louisa's obituary. The obituary (God bless that woman) states, "She was born in Appomattox Court House Virginia in 1837, a slave, on the plantation of Joel Flood, when Louisa was about 4 years of age. She married Charles Anderson in 1857 when she moved to Lynchburg, Virginia." This obituary is misleading because the dates and information don't correspond to what probably happened. It's unlikely she moved to Lynchburg in 1857 because she still would have been enslaved. It's more likely the date should be 1867, after the end of slavery. The reference about Louisa being four years old is a detail I can't reconcile.

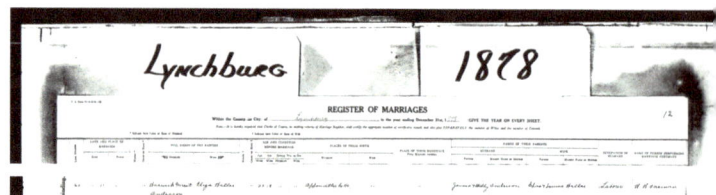

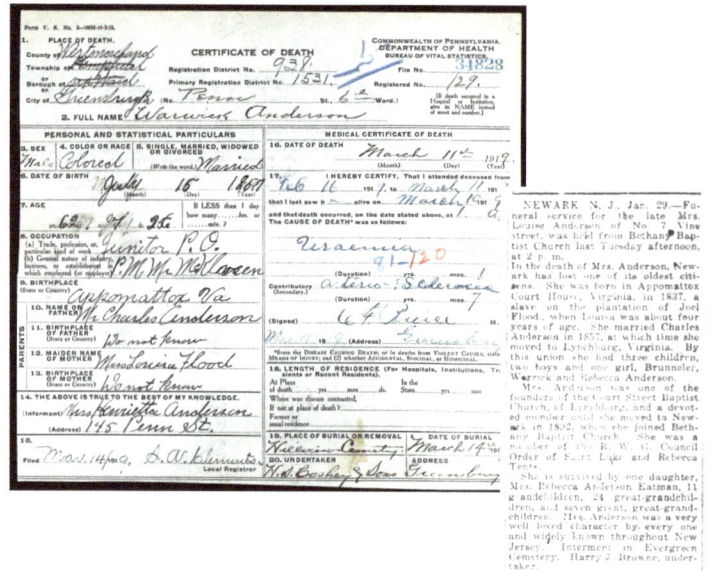

Surname Tree
FLOOD

Louise Flood
1837–1925

Warrick Garret Anderson Sr.
1857–1919

Warwick Waller Anderson Jr.
1885–1937

Helen Anderson
1916–1935

Jean Mae "Skeema" Anderson
1934–1984

This obituary provides many useful pieces of information. One, my assumption about the formerly enslaved taking their enslaver's last names was accurate. Two, the obituary confirms my hunch that Louisa Flood had three children. Three, the obituary lists the enslaver's name, and from there, it was simple to find him.

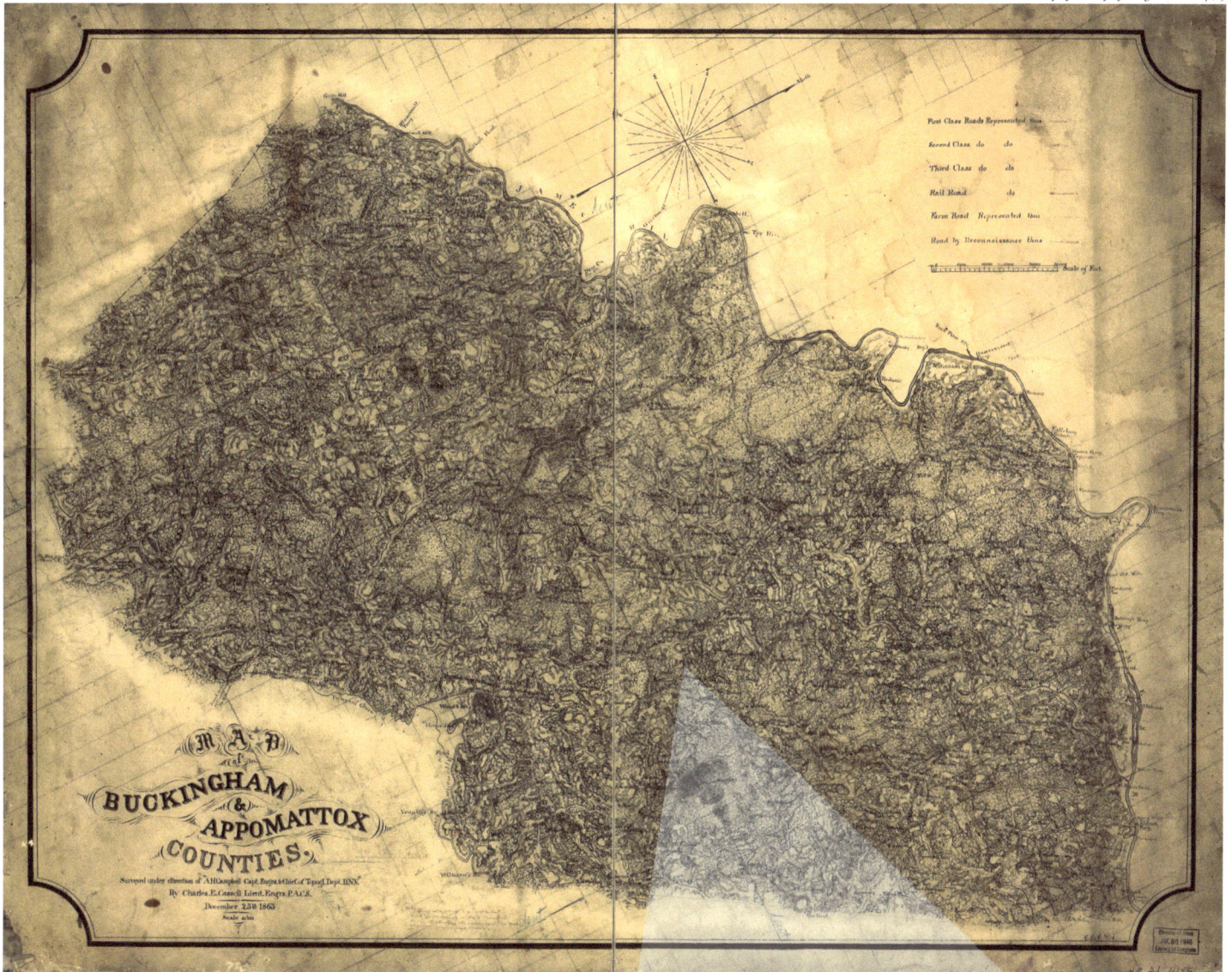

I was able to find pictures and a map showing the approximate location of the plantation. I requested Louisa Flood Anderson's death certificate from the New Jersey Office of Vital Records, which listed her mother as Rebecca. This is a significant throughline, because her daughter was also named Rebecca.

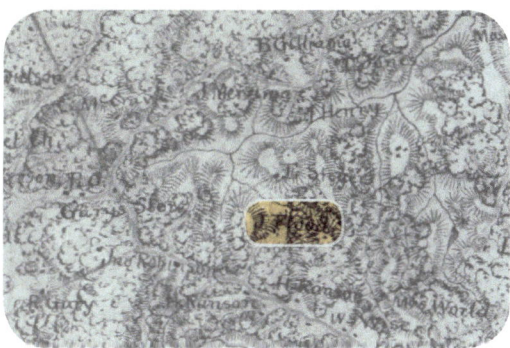

A cursory look at Joel Flood, Rebecca's mother's enslaver, reveals a man whose family fought in the Revolutionary and Civil Wars and served in the Virginia Legislature and Congress. The Flood patriarch, John Flood, arrived from England around 1754 and received an Albemarle County, VA, land patent (or deed) in 1760 for about 290 acres of land. Until the end of the Civil War, the Flood family oversaw at least 83 enslaved persons and had over 5,000 acres of land, an area slightly smaller than Williamsburg, VA. I hoped to find a mention of our ancestors in a will from Joel Flood's parents, but since Appomattox County, VA, is a burned county, the will does not exist.

1853 Appomattox County, VA land tax record

Burned counties may seem like a dead end, but they can actually help track formerly enslaved people. Louisa Flood's obituary told me where she was in 1867. Even without the obituary, I could still have tried to track her for the five years between the end of slavery and the 1870 census. Personal and land tax records, delinquent tax lists, court documents, and newspaper articles about court cases can all be useful resources.

Enslaver Surname:	**Location:**
Harris/Nicholas	*Albemarle County, VA*

ETYMOLOGY OF "HARRIS"

English (southern England and south Wales): from the personal name Harry + genitival -s, this surname is also common in Ireland beginning with the Plantation of Ulster.

ETYMOLOGY OF "NICHOLAS"

From Latin NICOLAUS from Greek NIKOLAOS (from NIKAN, 'to conquer' + LAOS 'people')

NICHOLAS PLANTATION STATISTICS

6 Cows

50 Sheep

70 Swine

Hay 3 tons

Butter 300 lbs

Wheat 350 bushels

Corn 850 bushels

Oats 100 bushels

Potatoes 20 bushels

Wool 100 lbs

Bees 100 lbs

Peas/Beans 3 bushels

Sweet Potatoes 20 bushels

Flax 10 lbs

Tobacco 7000 lbs

IMPROVED LAND 400 ACRES

UNIMPROVED LAND 450 ACRES

Jean Mae Anderson's maternal great-great-grandmother, Martha Harris, was born around 1848 and died after 1900. The first post-Civil War census shows her in Albemarle County, VA, specifically in St. Anne's Parish. She was married to Carter Nicholas.

Surname Tree
NICHOLAS/HARRIS

William Carter Nicholas
1815 - 1900

Martha Harris
1848 - 1865

Helen Nicholas
1865 - 1933

Lucinda Powell
1886 - 1929

Helen Anderson
1916 - 1935

Jean Mae
"Skeema" Anderson
1934 - 1984

Through the 1860 Slave Schedule and census, I found John H. Nicholas, who also lived in St. Anne's Parish, and I noticed his middle name was Harris.

When John H. Nicholas' maternal grandfather, William Harris, passed away in 1815, his mother, Frances "Fanny" Harris, and her siblings received negroes in the will. I surmise that the descendants of one of those slaves was Martha Harris.

William Harris's will

Sons were frequently given their mother's maiden name as their middle name. After she married Lewis Valentine Nicholas, Frances "Fanny" Harris named her son John Harris Nicholas.

TABLE OF TRACTS OF LAND FOR THE YEAR 1865

In Albemarle County, within the District of James H. Fry, Commissioner of the Revenue, with Taxes thereon at forty cents on every hundred dollars value thereof.

21

LOOKING THROUGH LAND TAX RECORDS IT LED ME TO BELIEVE THAT JOHN HARRIS NICHOLAS IS THE OWNER OF WILLIAM CARTER NICHOLAS. HIS FARM WAS VERY NEAR TO THE POWELL FARM (HELEN NICHOLAS MARRIED LEONARD POWELL) AND THE LAND TAX RECORDS LIST THE NAMES OF THE POWELL & NICHOLAS PROPERTIES AS "GREEN CREEK"

The land tax records for John Harris Nicholas list a property named Green Creek, 25 miles south of the Albemarle Courthouse. Using the AncestryDNA® ThruLines® of Jean Mae Anderson's half-brother, I determined that he was related to the descendants of a man named Wilson Nicholas. Wilson Nicholas is a full brother to John H. Nicholas, and common sense says they share a common ancestor. Given the centimorgans, the most probable shared ancestor is Lewis Valentine Nicholas, the white father of William Carter Nicholas, Martha Harris' husband. I fastidiously try to back up my claims in this book with factual evidence, but sometimes that evidence is no longer available. I confirmed the DNA connection through AncestryDNA® ThruLines®. However, the evidence is no longer available, because the relative who connected to Wilson Nicholas on Ancestry.com removed or made their DNA profile private. When this happens, you can no longer see how people are connected.

I've included this unconfirmed link to illustrate the importance of keeping accurate records and detailing sources to support your claims. I wrote my conclusions in my genealogy log book without stating whose DNA connected with our families. This saga shows how the landscape can change while you're researching and the importance of keeping detailed notes. This specific example has wider implications, because Lewis Valentine Nicholas came from a prominent family, and his brother Wilson Cary Nicholas was a governor of Virginia who was a neighbor and friend of Thomas Jefferson. Wilson Cary Nicholas' daughter, Jane Hollins Nicholas, married Thomas Jefferson's grandson, Thomas Jefferson Randolph, thus connecting that part of the Nicholas family to the third president of the United States. This does *not* mean the descendants of William Carter Nicholas are related to Thomas Jefferson, but it does illustrate the interwoven nature of families and properties in the 19th century. This example also shows the importance of ensuring someone actually belongs on your family tree.

I should mention that the Nicholas story would have been shorter without the DNA evidence, which further proves the accuracy of my notes. Using only historical records, I would have concluded that John Harris Nicholas was the enslaver of William Carter Nicholas. Adding his father, Lewis Valentine Nicholas, or brother, Wilson Nicholas, wouldn't have produced additional genealogical insights. I was also hesitant to unnecessarily expand the family trees of our enslavers. I am confident that my claims will be proven true as more descendants of Lewis Valentine Nicholas add their DNA to Ancestry.com.

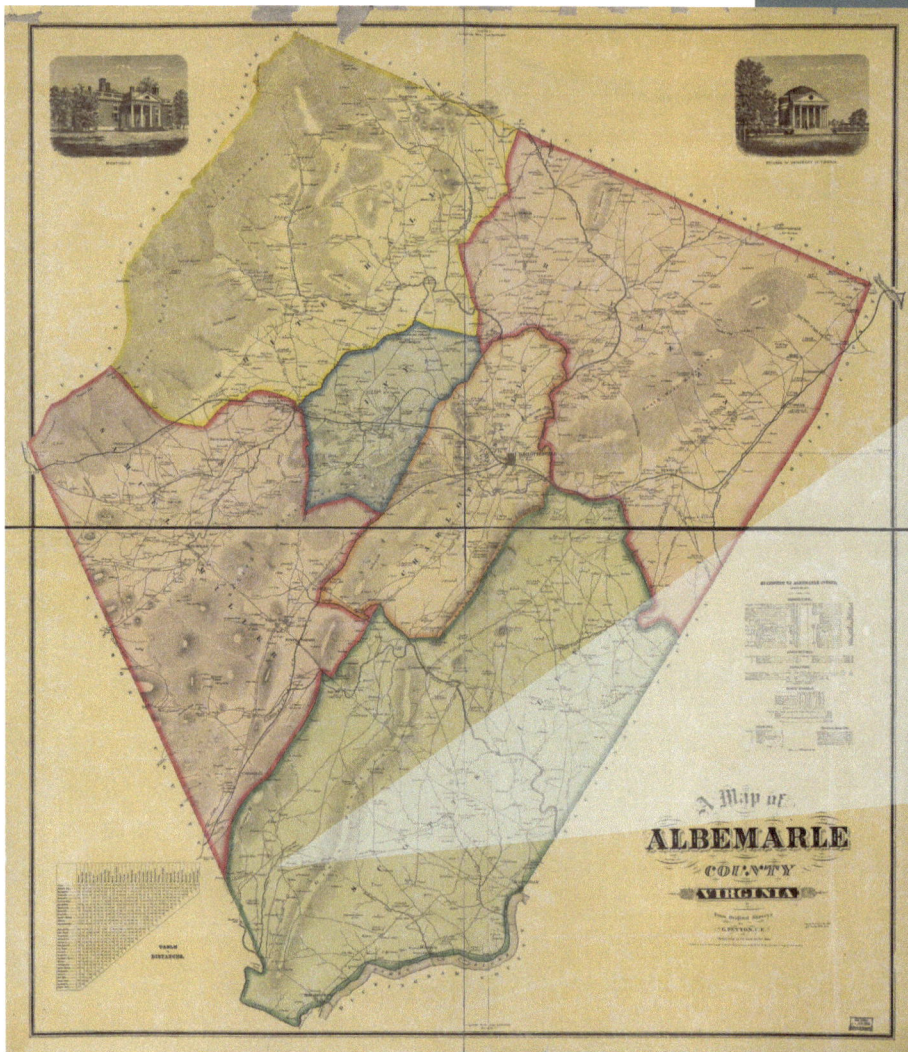

Courtesy of Library of Congress, 2013626350

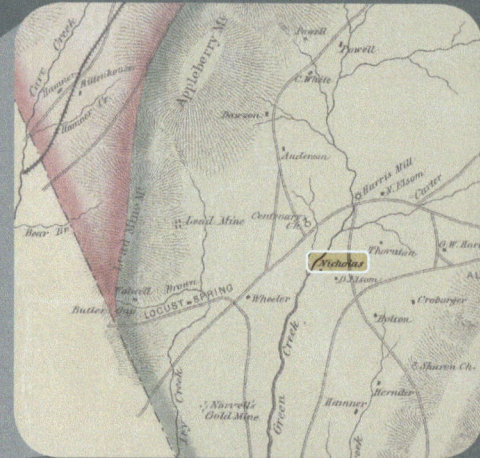

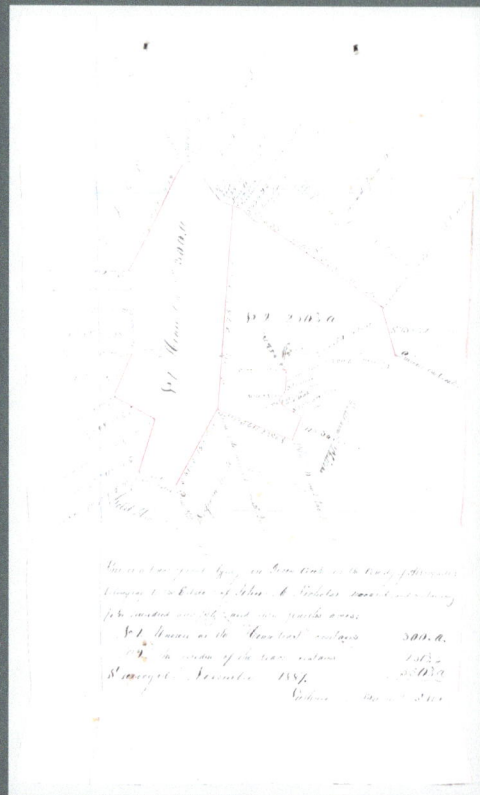

Courtesy of Library of Virginia

The Nicholas estate in the southern part of Albemarle County, VA, occupied more than 750 acres. The map shows some of their neighbors, such as the Powells and Harrises. This further strengthens my claims of the connectedness of the Harris and Nicholas families in particular, because our ancestors married people that were geographically close. This map was a wonderful discovery from the Libraries of Virginia and Congress. Cartographers included the names of landowners, and those additions helped me narrow down the location of our enslaved ancestors. Determining the exact location of a plantation can be challenging, but it's not impossible. Before permanent addresses were established, a property was located according to the direction and distance from the county courthouse. The Nicholas property, 25 miles southeast of the Albemarle County, VA courthouse, was surveyed using the "metes and bounds" method. Instead of longitude or latitude coordinates, property lines were demarcated by natural landmarks such as rocks, fallen trees, or bodies of water.

During litigation over John H. Nicholas' estate, I found this survey plat in the chancery records. While most of the "markers" are presently unidentifiable, the presence of the Green Creek could help modern-day sleuths find the exact location of the plantation.

ETYMOLOGY OF "POWELL"

Welsh: anglicized form of Welsh AP HYWEL (son of HYWEL), a personal name meaning "eminent."

Irish: sometimes a surname adopted as the equivalent of Gaelic MAC GIOLLA PHOIL (son of the servant of ST. PAUL).

POWELL PLANTATION STATISTICS

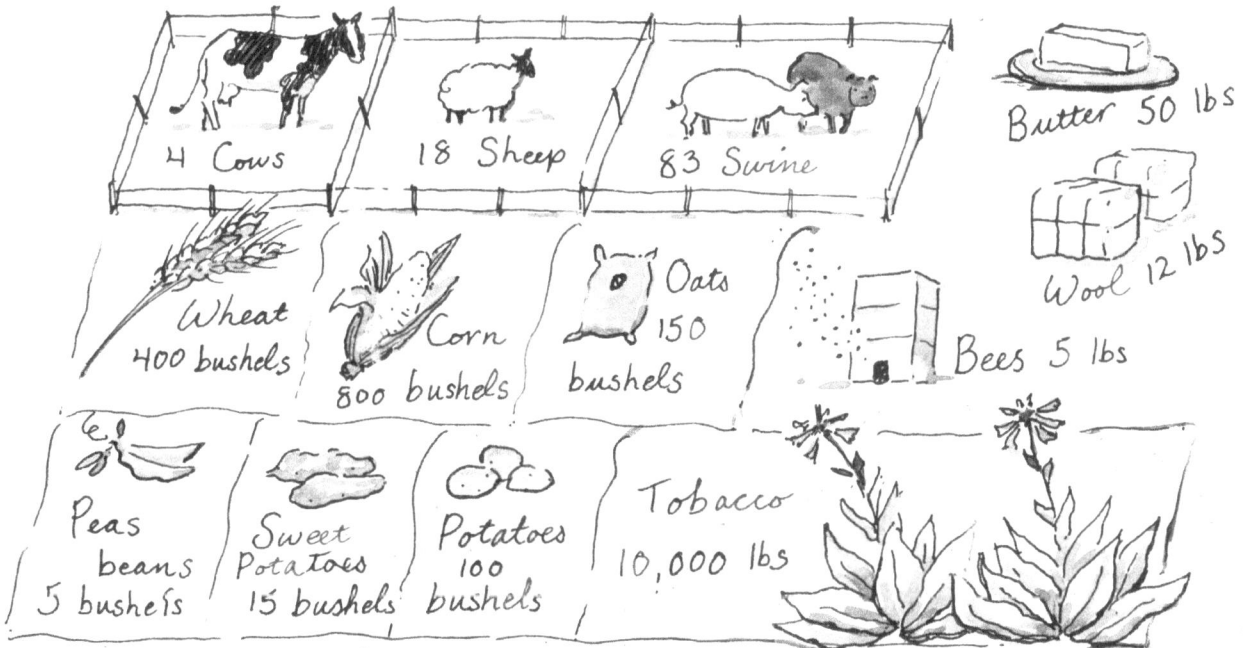

4 Cows

18 Sheep

83 Swine

Butter 50 lbs

Wool 12 lbs

Wheat 400 bushels

Corn 800 bushels

Oats 150 bushels

Bees 5 lbs

Peas beans 5 bushels

Sweet Potatoes 15 bushels

Potatoes 100 bushels

Tobacco 10,000 lbs

IMPROVED LAND 300 ACRES

UNIMPROVED LAND 150 ACRES

Surname Tree
POWELL

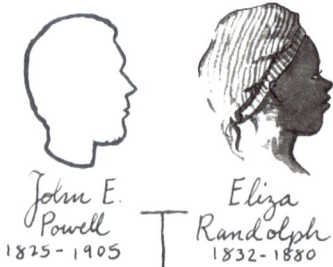

John E. Powell
1875 – 1905

Eliza Randolph
1832 – 1880

Leonard Randolph Powell
1862 – 1929

Lucinda Powell
1886 – 1929

Helen Anderson
1916 – 1935

Jean Mae "Skeema" Anderson
1934 – 1984

Leonard Randolph Powell is Jean Mae Anderson's maternal great-grandfather, and his death certificate lists his parents as John E. Powell and Eliza Powell. In the 1870 census, Leonard is listed as a Mulatto living with his mother Eliza Randolph and his eight siblings in Rockfish, Nelson County, VA, and next door, a white man named John E. Powell. If John E. Powell was his father, why was he living next door, and why had Eliza assumed the last name "Randolph"?

I discovered that of Leonard's eight siblings, John E. and Eliza Powell, were listed as parents on five marriage certificates and three death certificates and as "friend" on one birth register.

This John E. Powell was born in Albemarle County, VA, a slaveholder who served in the Confederate Army. John E. Powell's activities are recorded in a census, property tax document, and maps.

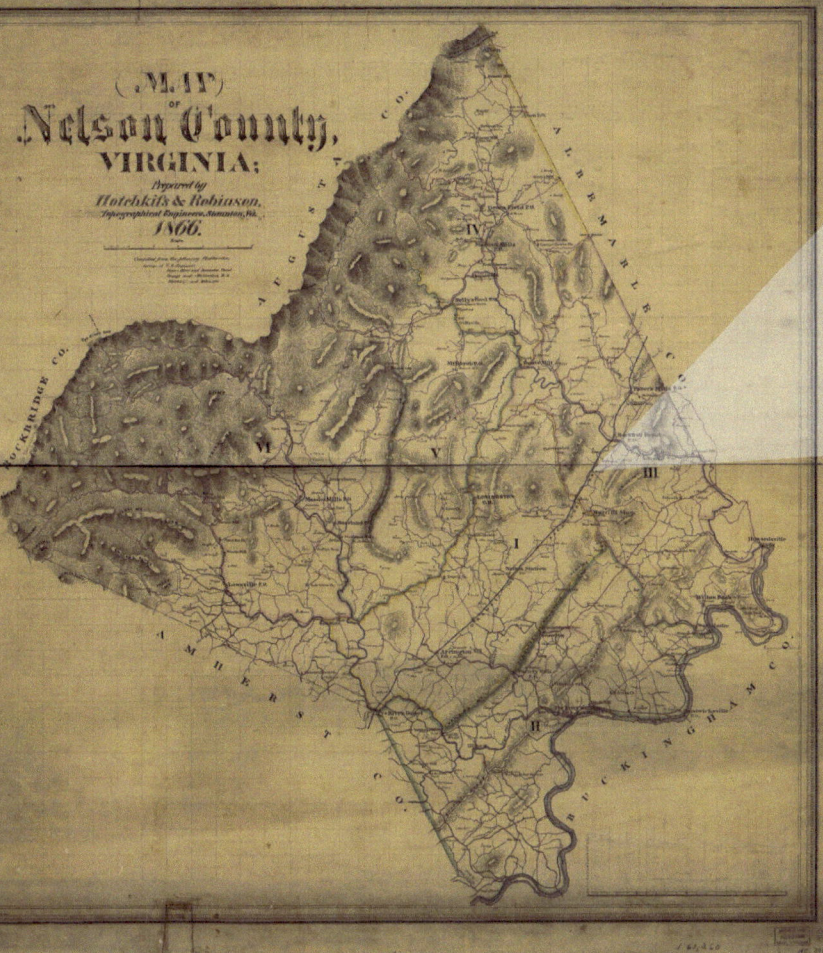

Courtesy of the Library of Congress, 2005625585

He frequently appears in records alongside an older Leonard Powell. John was listed with Leonard as an overseer, and given the approximate 30-year age difference, it's probable that Leonard was his father's brother. John managed properties in both Albemarle and Nelson Counties, VA, under the tutelage of Leonard. When looking through county records, I frequently found references to Leonard Powell but not John E. Powell. At first, I discarded these mentions, but I've since learned that connecting secondary characters is just as valuable as searching for your target.

John E. Powell fathered children with Mulatto Eliza Randolph Powell from 1852 until 1870, five years after the end of slavery. I didn't trust the records, but through census and marriage records, I traced John E. Powell's journey through Rockfish, Nelson County, VA, to Lovingston, Nelson County, Virginia, and his eventual marriage to Edmonia Warren, a white woman, in 1888.

John E. Powell
1825–1905

Isaac J. Powell
1852–1934

Eliza Randolph Powell
1856–1943

Charity Powell
1860–1932

Leonard R Powell
1862–1929

Alexander Powell
1864–

Sallie Powell
1885–1981

William Andrew Powell
1892–1970

I was doubtful John E. Powell was the father to Mulatto Eliza Randolph Powell's children until I discovered AncestryDNA matches for John E. Powell's descendants. The DNA proof is incontrovertible: Eliza Randolph's children and Edmonia's children are all related to John E. Powell. John E. Powell provided for Edmonia and their nine children while presiding over 1,848 acres of landholdings across two counties (Albemarle and Nelson) until his death, when his will seemingly divided his estate among his white heirs.

Courtesy of Library of Virginia

After John E. Powell's death, his heirs discovered that he had an unpaid debt to Emily Thomas and her children. His widow, Edmonia, sued for a portion of her husband's estate. Additionally, there were multiple unrecorded wills, and John had previously sold some of the estate he had bequeathed to his heirs. Edmonia Powell eventually received a third of her husband's estate, which included some land and a house.

An overseer was an individual who supervised the plantation operations, especially in regards to enslaved people.

This illustrates a common part of ancestry research. I had previously found John E. Powell's will and how he'd generously divided his estate amongst his white children. Further research gave a fuller story, showing that he was financially insecure and made unwise business decisions that nearly left his white family without land or a home. Some may believe that white enslavers sat on buckets of money that were passed from generation to generation, but most of their wealth was in tangible items such as land, slaves, livestock, farm tools, and household items. When John E. Powell passed, he had $415 in the bank. The rest of his estate consisted of land, plantation tools, and furniture.

ETYMOLOGY OF "FONTAINE"

French and Walloon: topographic name for someone living near a spring or a well, of from Old French FONTAINE; the name of several places in various parts of France.

Spelling was not as important in the nineteenth century as today. It was common for people to write a word phonetically, which allows for multiple spellings of the same name or word to proliferate. Although "Fountain" is used in vital records, I strongly believe this is a misspelling of "Fontaine".

I don't include the Fontaine family to illustrate what I've discovered but rather to explain how discoveries don't always lead to conclusions. One of my assumptions was that an ancestor did not move from 1865 to 1870. But that assumption becomes doubtful if you don't have the 1870 census. I have the 1880 census that mentions Mollie Fountain, where she and her family are listed as being in Black Walnut, Halifax County, VA.

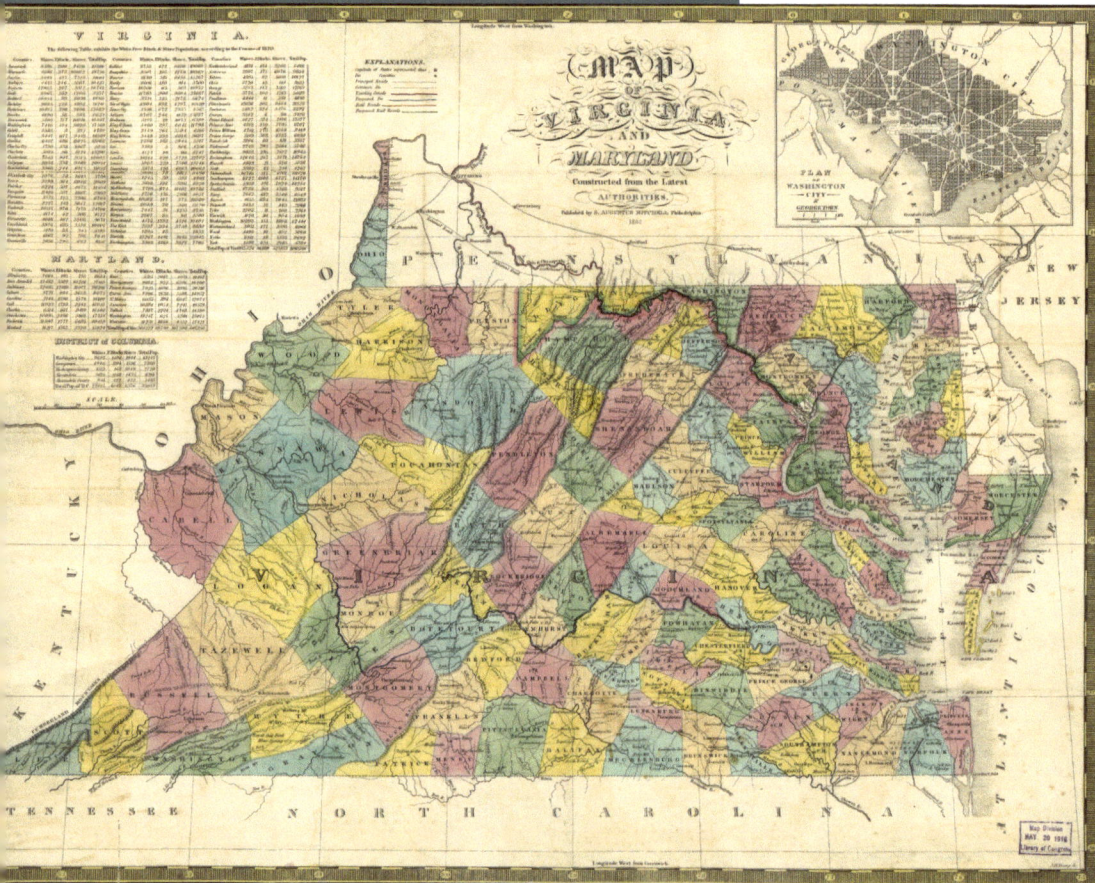

Looking through the 1860 census and slave schedules, I found Fontaine slaveholders in Buckingham, Fluvanna, Goochland, Hanover, Henry, Pittsylvania, King William, and Wythe Counties, but none in Halifax County. This is despite Halifax County survey plats being available for Moses and Peter Fontaine and without any indication that those assets were sold or transferred. Halifax County is close to these counties, and it isn't unreasonable to believe that the enslaved lived on a plantation in one county and then migrated to Halifax County in the fifteen years after the end of the Civil War. Unfortunately, without more information, it isn't possible to know which plantation our ancestors came from.

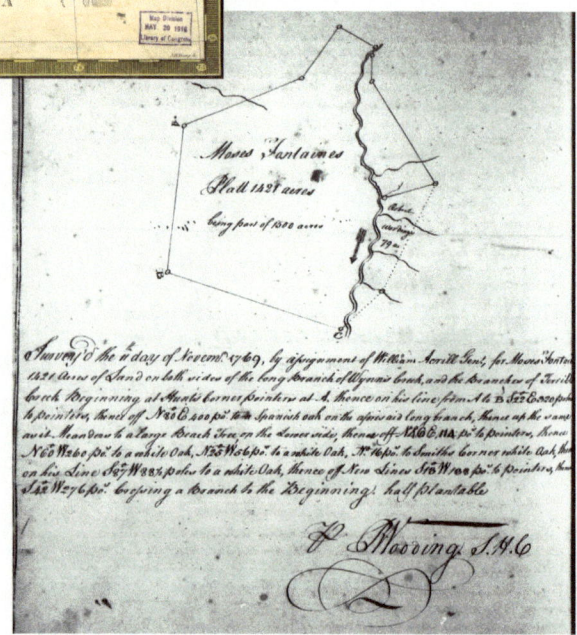

During this research, I was able to recreate the Fontaine tree and determine who was related to whom, but I still couldn't connect them to our family. Maybe this link will appear with more research. After all, new records are discovered all the time!

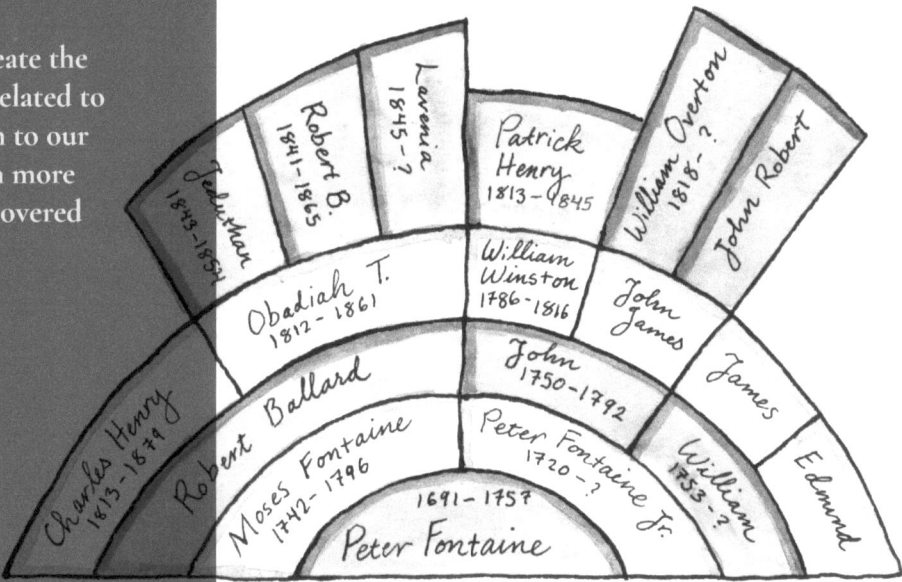

Fan chart names: Jeduthan 1843-1854 · Robert B. 1841-1865 · Lavenia 1845-? · Patrick Henry 1813-1845 · William Overton 1818-? · John Robert · Obadiah T. 1812-1861 · William Winston 1786-1816 · John James · Charles Henry 1813-1874 · Robert Ballard · Moses Fontaine 1742-1796 · John 1750-1792 · Peter Fontaine Jr. 1720-? · James · William 1753-? · Edmund · Peter Fontaine 1691-1757

Not only do we discover new records, but we can also reexamine existing records to look for fresh insights or different conclusions. For example, I was frustrated that I couldn't find a mention of Nathan Fountain with his family in the 1870 census. This would have helped me identify his enslaver. I've read historical records about how the federal government went to extraordinary lengths to account for formerly enslaved people after the Civil War. It is possible that the Fountain family had been missed, though this was not very common.

I revisited the records I'd saved for Nathan Fountain, Mollie Fountain's father. The 1870 census listed a Nathan Fountain with the Betts family, but I had disregarded this document. I assumed this wasn't the Nathan Fountain I was tracking until I used AncestryDNA® ThruLines® and discovered his descendants were related to members of the Betts family. The Betts descended from Charlotte Fountain Betts, likely Nathan Fountain's sister.

Two additional details eventually helped me piece together this puzzle and conclude that no one was missing. In fact, I had misinterpreted the records. To begin with, Nathan Fountain and his future wife Nancy Fultz weren't listed together in the 1870 census because they hadn't yet established a household together. Nathan is listed with his sister, and Nancy with her mother, Harriet Fultz. The second detail is that Mollie Fountain was 10 years old in the 1880 census. She was probably not included in the 1870 census because she had not been born yet. The simplicity of the solution makes perfect sense, but overlooking Mollie Fountain's age blinded me to the veracity of the records.

While unraveling this mystery, I delved deeper into the white Fontaine family. I connected some Fontaines to Halifax County, VA, and I found repositories of Fontaine family records that I had missed. These documents are at the Library of Virginia, the Virginia Museum of History and Culture, and the University of Texas at Austin. There were also some at the Library of Congress and Daughters of the American Revolution. I am optimistic that these collections will help me get to the bottom of the Fontaine surname. These records aren't digitized, so I'll visit these libraries in person to complete the Fontaine/Fountain family tree.

ETYMOLOGY OF PENICK

Welsh: perhaps a nickname from Middle English PENNOC ("big-headed" or "with a large head"), possibly "headstrong")

English (mainly North Yorkshire) perhaps from an unrecorded Middle English personal name PENOC, which might be a pet form of Old English PÆGNA, of uncertain origin.

PENICK PLANTATION STATISTICS

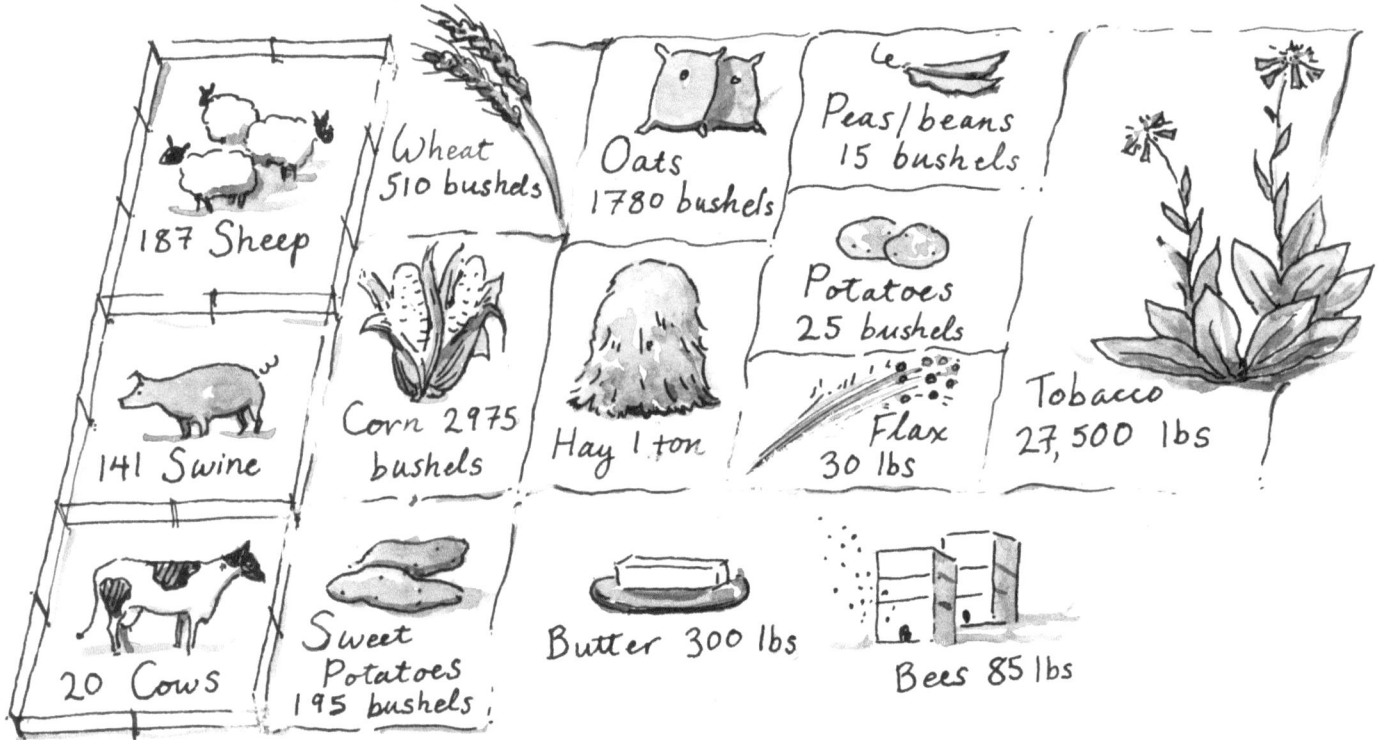

187 Sheep

141 Swine

20 Cows

Wheat 510 bushels

Corn 2975 bushels

Sweet Potatoes 195 bushels

Oats 1780 bushels

Hay 1 ton

Butter 300 lbs

Peas/beans 15 bushels

Potatoes 25 bushels

Flax 30 lbs

Bees 85 lbs

Tobacco 27,500 lbs

IMPROVED LAND 1100 ACRES

UNIMPROVED LAND 1144 ACRES

Surname Tree
PENICK

Richard Penick
DATES UNKNOWN

Edward Penick
1840 – ?

Edward Penick
1871 – ?

Robert Penick
1884 – 1935

John Robert Penick
1914 – 1967

Jean Mae "Skeema" Anderson
1934 – 1984

The Andersons never knew who her father was because Jean Mae's mother died from a gunshot wound when Jean Mae was three months old. In the spring of 2024, Jean Mae's grandson submitted his DNA to Ancestry.com, and a close link was established with a second cousin, Wendy Penick. It was confirmed that Wendy's father, Eugene Penick, was a half-brother of Jean Mae Anderson, whose father was John Robert Penick. This revelation opened a new branch to the Anderson tree; in addition to being an Anderson, Jean Mae was also a Penick.

DIES OF WOUND

Helen Anderson, Negro, who was shot through the neck February 18, died at Lynchburg Hospital at 3:45 o'clock yesterday. The shot severed her spinal cord, paralyzing the lower part of her body. Governor Turner, Negro, has been held in jail since the shooting, and may be charged with murder.

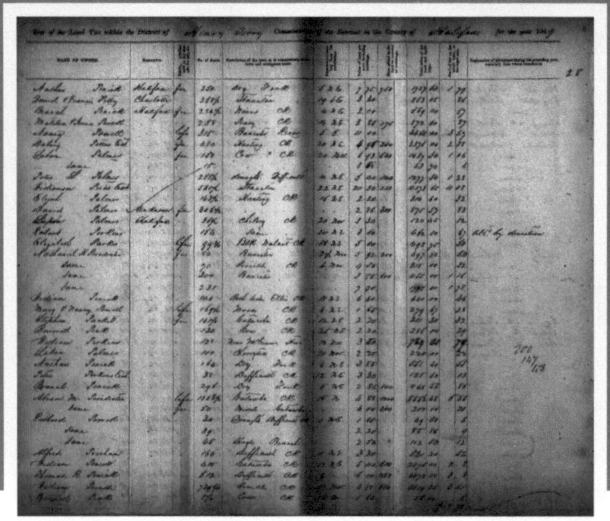

I built the Penick tree because I wanted to determine when the Penicks came to America and where and how they established a foothold in the colonies. Edward Penick (1670-1733) settled in Prince Edward County, VA, but his descendants gradually migrated through Hanover County into Halifax County, VA. In the 1860 Slave Schedule, Edward's great grandsons, Thomas R. and William Penick, were the only slaveholders in Halifax County. However, there was also a Nathan Penick in the adjacent county of Pittsylvania. Reviewing the property tax records, I also found a reference to a Branch Penick.

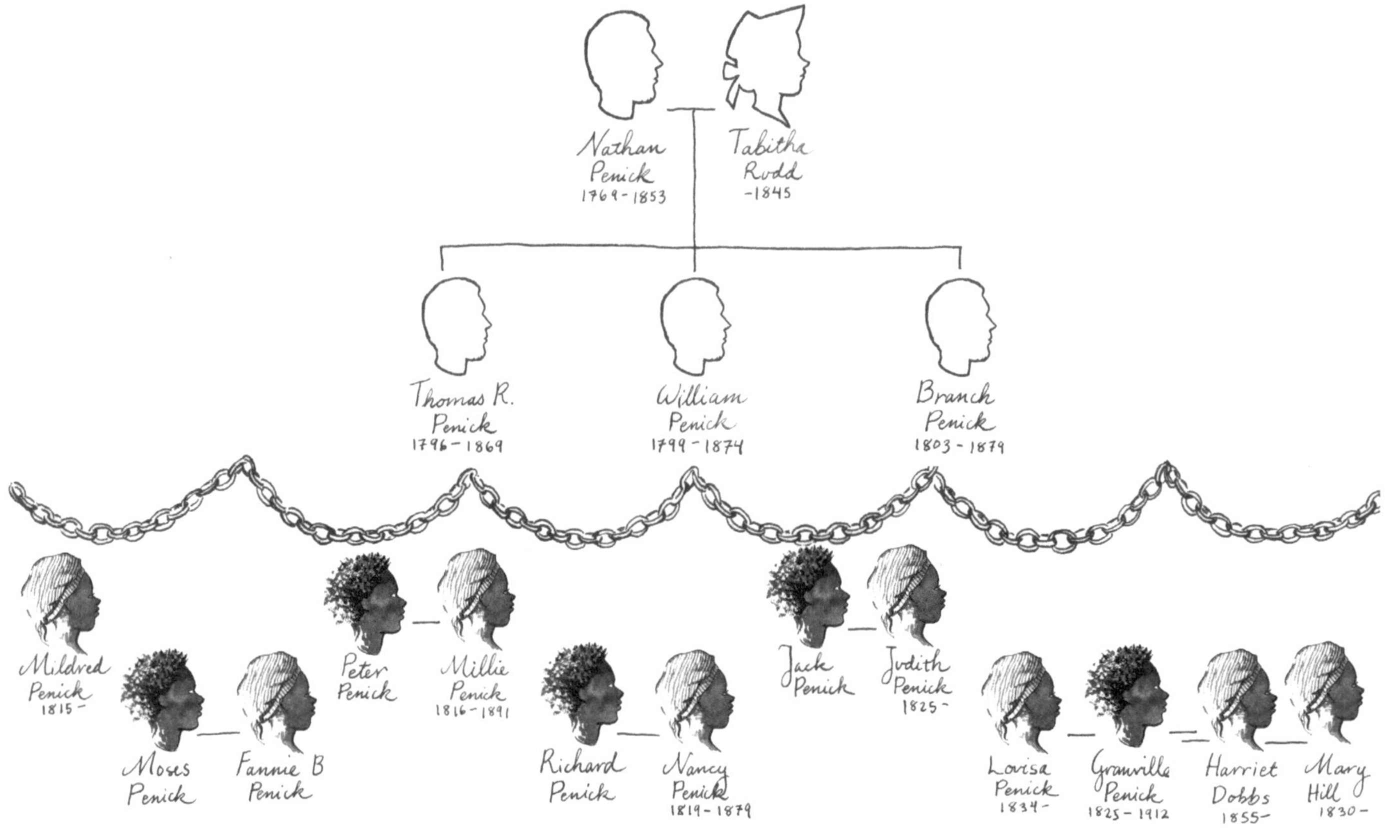

Nathan Penick
1769–1853

Tabitha Rodd
–1845

Thomas R. Penick
1796–1869

William Penick
1799–1874

Branch Penick
1803–1879

Mildred Penick
1815–

Moses Penick

Fannie B Penick

Peter Penick

Millie Penick
1816–1891

Richard Penick

Nancy Penick
1819–1879

Jack Penick

Judith Penick
1825–

Lovisa Penick
1834–

Granville Penick
1825–1912

Harriet Dobbs
1855–

Mary Hill
1830–

The Halifax Land tax records from 1846–1870 indicate the Penick family oversaw a total of 3,400 acres that were 4–18 miles northeast of the Halifax courthouse. The plantations bordered Wynn, Catawba, Difficult, Dry Fork, and Terrible Creeks, but I haven't been able to determine the exact location. The acres the Penicks were taxed for changed from year to year, so I'm not certain if they purchased and sold land to each other or to outside parties. However, we do know that their plantations were major producers. The Penick Plantation Statistics illustration shows one year's collective output of their massive plantations from the 1860 agriculture schedule.

As I researched the Penick family tree, I realized there are Penick branches that aren't linked by DNA or lineage but rather because they lived in the same time period. The oldest Penicks I found were Moses, Fannie B, Richard, Nancy, Mildred, Judith, and Millie . These Penicks were born between 1810–1825. I decided to place them together in a tree under the slaveholder Edward Penick's great-grandchildren. Thomas R., William, and Branch regularly appear in the records at the same location. It is most probable that our ancestors were enslaved by them and had their own individual family units while sharing continuous plots of land. Given the proximity of the oldest recorded Penicks to one another, it is possible that they were related by blood.

ETYMOLOGY OF "SHIPP"

English: nickname for a mariner or perhaps a boatbuilder from Middle English SCHIP (ship)

SHIPP PLANTATION STATISTICS

Wheat 40 bushels

Sweet Potatoes 15 bushels

Oats 120 bushels

Corn 150 bushels

Butter 25 lbs

Tobacco 5000 lbs

IMPROVED LAND
75 ACRES

UNIMPROVED LAND
175 ACRES

Ahhhh, the Shipps. This was a fun surname to research! Vital records brought me to Joseph Shipp, who I know was a white person because he's listed in the 1860 Slave Schedule as an owner. His status is further confirmed by the 1850 census, where he is listed as an overseer, and by his mother's extraordinary will. When Sarah Shipp died in 1853, she gave her son four negroes, one of whom was named Giles. To her daughter Lucinda, she bequeathed six negroes, one who was named Jane/Ginny. I believe Joseph Shipp, the white slaveholder, had children with Jane/Ginny Shipp, one of his sister's negroes. This conclusion is supported by Sarah Shipp's will, Giles Shipp's marriage, and death certificates listing Joseph and Ginny Shipp as Giles' parents. AncestryDNA testing also shows Joseph Shipp was the father of Giles and Fannie Shipp.

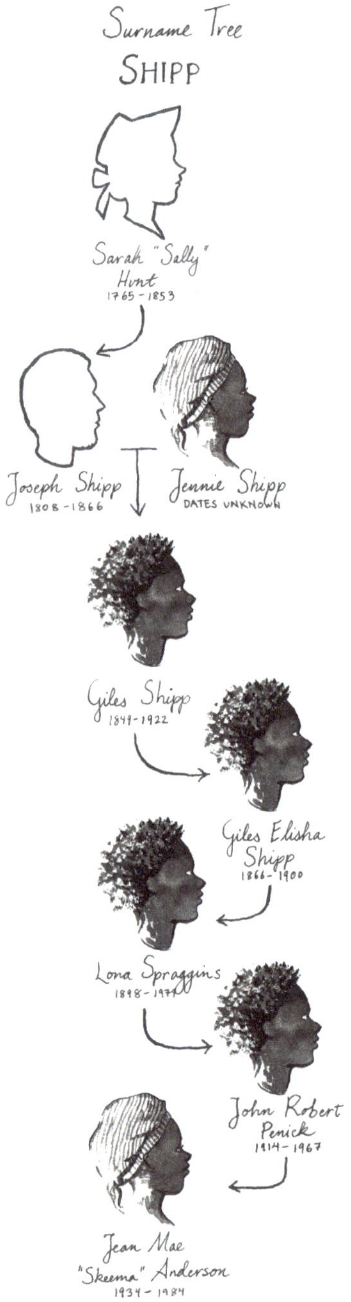

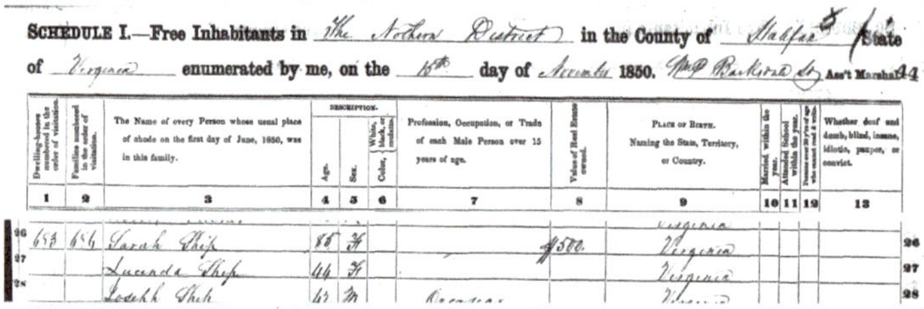

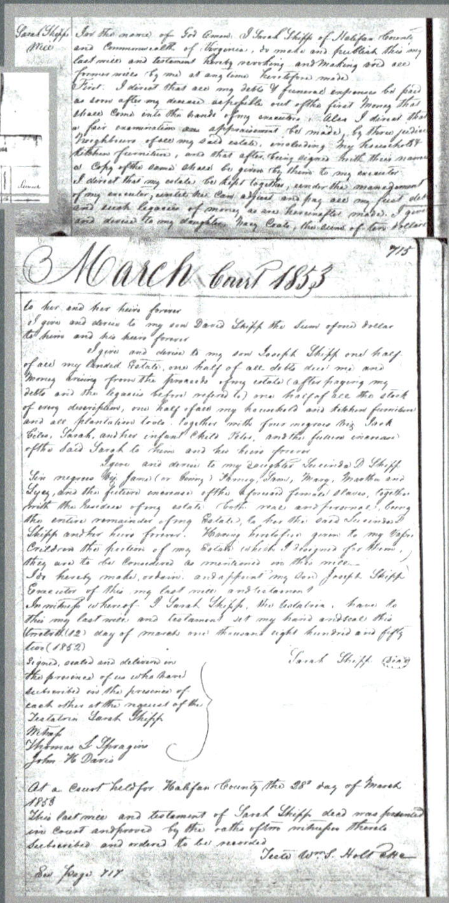

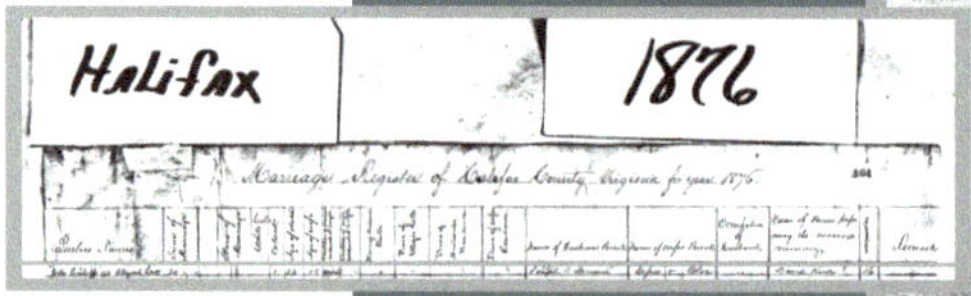

Surname Tree
SHIPP
Sarah "Sally" Hunt
1765 - 1853
Joseph Shipp
1808 - 1866
Jennie Shipp
DATES UNKNOWN
Giles Shipp
1849 - 1922
Giles Elisha Shipp
1866 - 1900
Lona Spraggins
1898 - 1974
John Robert Penick
1914 - 1967
Jean Mae "Skeema" Anderson
1934 - 1984

Page No. 45 — 320

SCHEDULE 2.—Slave Inhabitants in Nothern District in the County of Halifax State of Virginia, enumerated by me, on the 8th day of August, 1860. John H Taylor Ass't Marshal.

Joseph Shipp

SCHEDULE I.—Free Inhabitants in the Nothern District in the County of Halifax State of Virginia enumerated by me, on the 14th day of November 1850. Wm P Barksdale Ass't Marshal 44

Sarah Shipp — 85 — F — $500 — Virginia
Lucinda Shipp — 44 — F — Virginia
Joseph Shipp — 43 — M

Sarah Shipp's will

In the name of God Amen. I Sarah Shipp of Halifax County and Commonwealth of Virginia, do make and publish this my last will and testament hereby revoking and making void all former wills by me at any time heretofore made.

March Court 1853

Halifax — 1876

Marriage Register of Halifax County, Virginia for year 1876

CERTIFICATE OF DEATH
COMMONWEALTH OF VIRGINIA
24090

Place of death: Halifax — Staunton
Full name: Giles Shipp
Sex: Male — Color or race: Col'd — Married
Husband of: Susan Shipp
Age: 90
Occupation: none
Birthplace: Halifax Co.
Name of father: Joe Shipp
Birthplace of father: Va
Maiden name of mother: Unknown
Date of death: Nov 17 1922
Cause of death: Senility no definite disease
Informant: Jas. E. Poindexter, Nathalie
Burial: at Home — Nov 19 22
Undertaker: Paul Syann(?) — Nathalie Va
Filed Nov 18 1922 D. J. Merritt

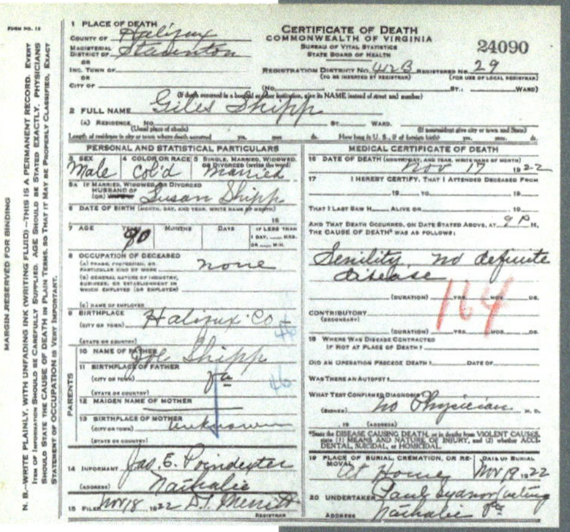

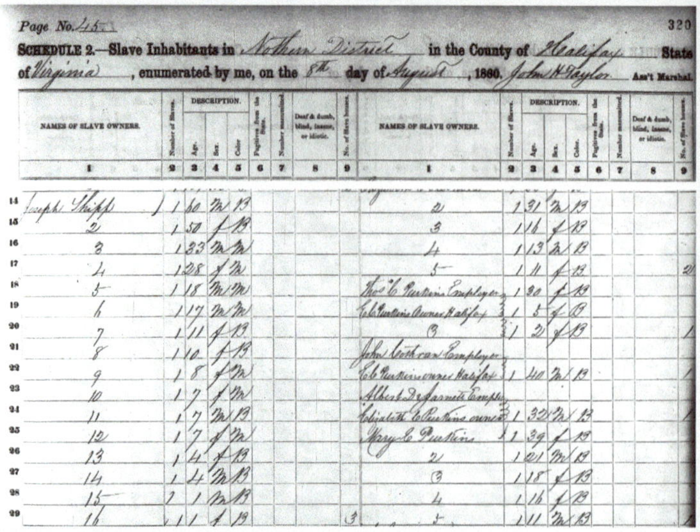

Sarah Shipp (née Hunt) was married twice, first to George Vasser and then to Thomas Shipp. These unions produced around nine children, and AncestryDNA® ThruLines® show Joseph and Jane/Ginny Shipp's great-great-great grandson, Eugene Penick, is related to all those descendants. Their common ancestor is Sarah Vasser Shipp (née Hunt), the mother of Joseph Shipp. Giles' identity is further supported by one of Sarah Shipp's neighbors, Thomas Lanier Spraggins. He drafted a memo outlining how to write Sarah's will and detailing the family relations of her slaves.

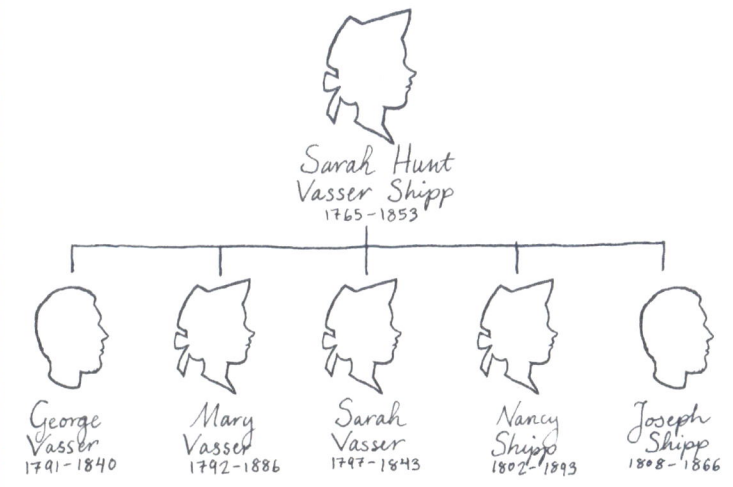

The Shipp property was located about 25 miles northwest of the Halifax County courthouse on a 250-acre tract of land named Bates Branch. Knowing that Joseph Shipp was a white man, I wanted to see if he included his colored family in his will. I first found Lucinda Shipp's (Joseph's sister) will, in which she left her entire estate to her brother Joseph, except for $1 for her brother David and sister Nancy. Even in 1857 dollars, this was a paltry sum. I discovered that her siblings contested the will, showing that they were litigious individuals.

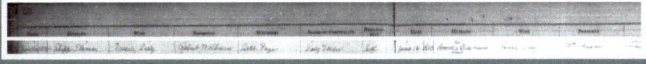

I continued to look for Joseph's will and narrowed his year of death to between 1860, when he appeared in the census, and 1867, when his estate was liquidated in a Halifax County will book. I scoured Halifax County will books from 1860–1869 and couldn't find a mention of his will. Then I thought that if his siblings contested Lucinda's will, maybe they had also contested Joseph's. I reviewed the Halifax County chancery records and found that his siblings had contested the absence of a will. They also claimed that Joseph intended to exclude his white siblings from his estate and leave everything to his colored family.

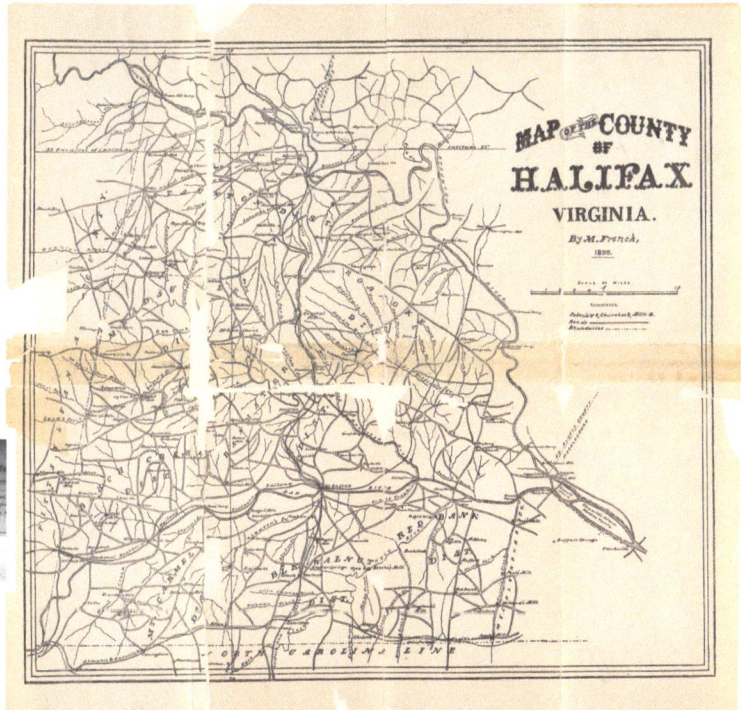

Nancy Beedles gave testimony during the will contestation, and I'd like to think this exchange about her husband might have produced a chuckle.

Over 100 documents read like a legal novel, as witnesses are deposed, and his siblings fight for a share of Joseph's estate. Not surprisingly, his white siblings prevailed, but the most thrilling records were the depositions of Lucy and Giles Shipp. For once, we can read our enslaved ancestors talking about who they are, what they did, and how they felt. We have the syntax of their speech and I was in awe that I could read historical documents from the 1870s and feel the words of my ancestors.

David Shipp and Nancy Coates (née Shipp) left modern-day researchers a gift, because they recorded Joseph Shipp's death on Nov. 7, 1866, from smallpox. Their petition to the court stated that Joseph did not have any heirs "...except negroes who had been his forever slaves" and that the absence of a will was because "...his house was burned to prevent the disease spreading." Over twenty people were deposed, and they repeatedly stated that Joseph didn't want this white family to receive his estate, preferring to bequeath his estate to his colored family.

Lucy Shipp's 1876 deposition describes how she had known Joseph Shipp all her life because her mother belonged to him. She states he made a will before he died, and she attested to that fact because she had seen it. Lucy said she could read but could not read the will "...because I can't read writing". I assume she is referring to reading cursive writing.

Giles Shipp was deposed on Aug. 23, 1876, and the seven-page account starts with him listing his age as 32. He confirms that his father didn't have any family other than "...his colored people, who were my mother and her children." Giles lived about ¾ of a mile from his father and took care of Joseph in his last days because he had previously had smallpox and was immune to the disease. When Joseph died, Giles said he and another man, Joel Brown, took all the papers from the house and gave them to James Calloway, Joseph's estate administrator. He repeats his sister's claim that Joseph's wish was to "...will his property to us, his colored people".

Portions of what is mentioned in this section can be found in the depositions. The full depositions can be found in the Appendix.

ETYMOLOGY OF "SPRAGGINS"

English: from an unrecorded Middle English personal name SPRAGIN, SPRAKIN, a pet form of SPRAG.

SPRAGGINS PLANTATION STATISTICS

10 Cows

170 Sheep

130 Swine

Wheat 400 bushels

Corn 1500 bushels

Flax 15 lbs

Wool 100 lbs

Hay 2 tons

Butter 700 lbs

Tobacco 17,500

IMPROVED LAND 800 ACRES

UNIMPROVED LAND 1000 ACRES

After most likely migrating from Northumberland, England, in the mid-1600s, the (white) Spraggins settled in Halifax County, VA, as early as 1757. There are references to several landmarks about 15-20 miles north of the county courthouse, such as Morton's Ferry Road, Bull Creek, Catawba Creek, Stokes Creeks, Dan River, Bates Branch, and Staunton properties. It is most probable that Thomas Lanier Spraggins and his father Melchizadek Spraggins, were the enslavers of the African American Spraggins.

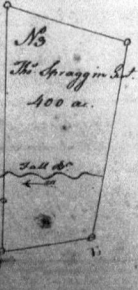

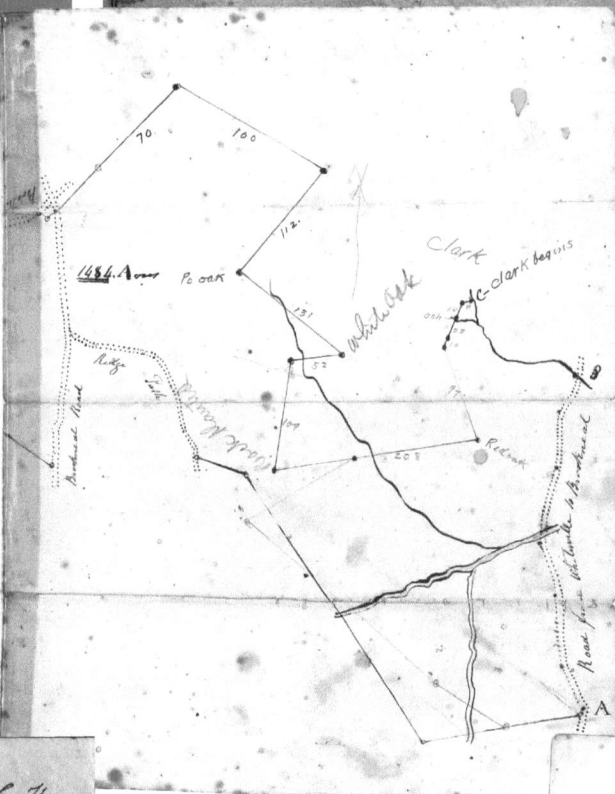

Courtesy of Virginia Museum of History & Culture (Mss1 Sp716b)

Clark Spraggins Family Papers (#440), East Carolina Manuscript Collection, J.Y. Joyner Library, East Carolina University, Greenville, North Carolina, USA.

The Thomas L. Spraggins documents reveal a "typical" antebellum enslaver. I only have access to the records that have survived, and it's possible that documentation showing a different side of Thomas L. Spraggins may be lost. He was a family man who kept track of the births and deaths of his family while selling negroes and separating *their* families. His farm operations focused on tobacco, because unlike other plantations, he didn't dabble in other agricultural products such as sweet potatoes or oats. I can't help but think that being enslaved on the Spraggins plantation was a hardship, more so than other plantations.

Melchizadek Spraggins and Thomas L. Spraggins died in 1810 and 1863, respectively. Their wills would have been taken to the Halifax County courthouse, and the wills' witnesses would have also gone to have the will proved. Once recorded at the courthouse, an executor would have been assigned. This was usually the son of the deceased person, but it was sometimes the wife or another interested party. After this, three things would happen. First, court-assigned inventory managers would catalog the assets of the deceased person's estate. If the wife was still alive, she received a third of the estate. Finally, the death would be published in the newspaper or posted in a notice outside the courthouse. If the deceased had any debts, these could be repaid with their estate's assets.

The will listed the heirs and what property, including enslaved persons, each heir should receive. If the heirs didn't want to manage their inheritance, the estate would pass through a chancery court of equity. This was a civil court that focused on fairness and equity rather than following the letter of the law. This court often handled divorces and estate, land, and business disputes. Court-assigned commissioners reviewed the evidence of the case and decided on a reasonable settlement. For a will, the commissioner would first use the assets to pay any outstanding debts. The commissioner would then either divide the estate among the heirs or liquidate the assets and deliver the proceeds to the heirs.

At the chancery, court records were divided into four parts:

Petition	The bill of complaint or the reason for the case
Answer	The response to the petition
Decree	The decision made by the judge (chancery cases didn't have juries)
Evidence	Such as depositions, correspondence, contested wills, plats, subpoenas, affidavits, receipts, or other pertinent documentation

Building trees for people seemingly unrelated to your ancestors is labor-intensive but sometimes necessary. Thomas L. Spraggins' deceased wife, Elizabeth Baker, received an inheritance from her father, Brooks Baker. In Baker's will, the enslaved Burrell and Martha are mentioned. They later appear in Thomas L. Spraggins' will.

The Library of Virginia's Chancery Records Index has 128 Sprag(g)ins family records. For genealogists, these cases are a valuable paper trail that provide numerous opportunities for us to locate our ancestors. Of course, not all of the cases involve the wills and estate inventories of Thomas and Melchizadek Spraggins, but it is necessary to look at each record to see if it is relevant. For example, an 1882 chancery case involving Thomas Spraggins' estate disbursement has 111 pages and mentions enslaved people Rally (Raleigh), Burwell, and Martha. I will need to review all these files to see if these people are my ancestors.

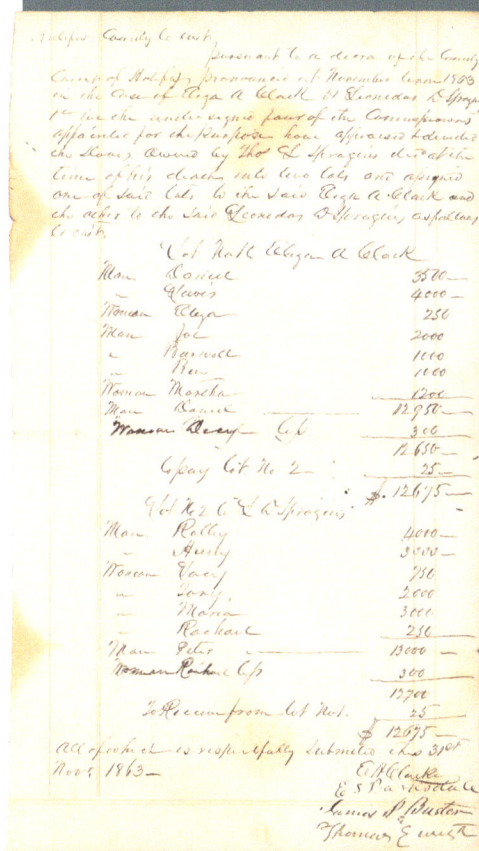

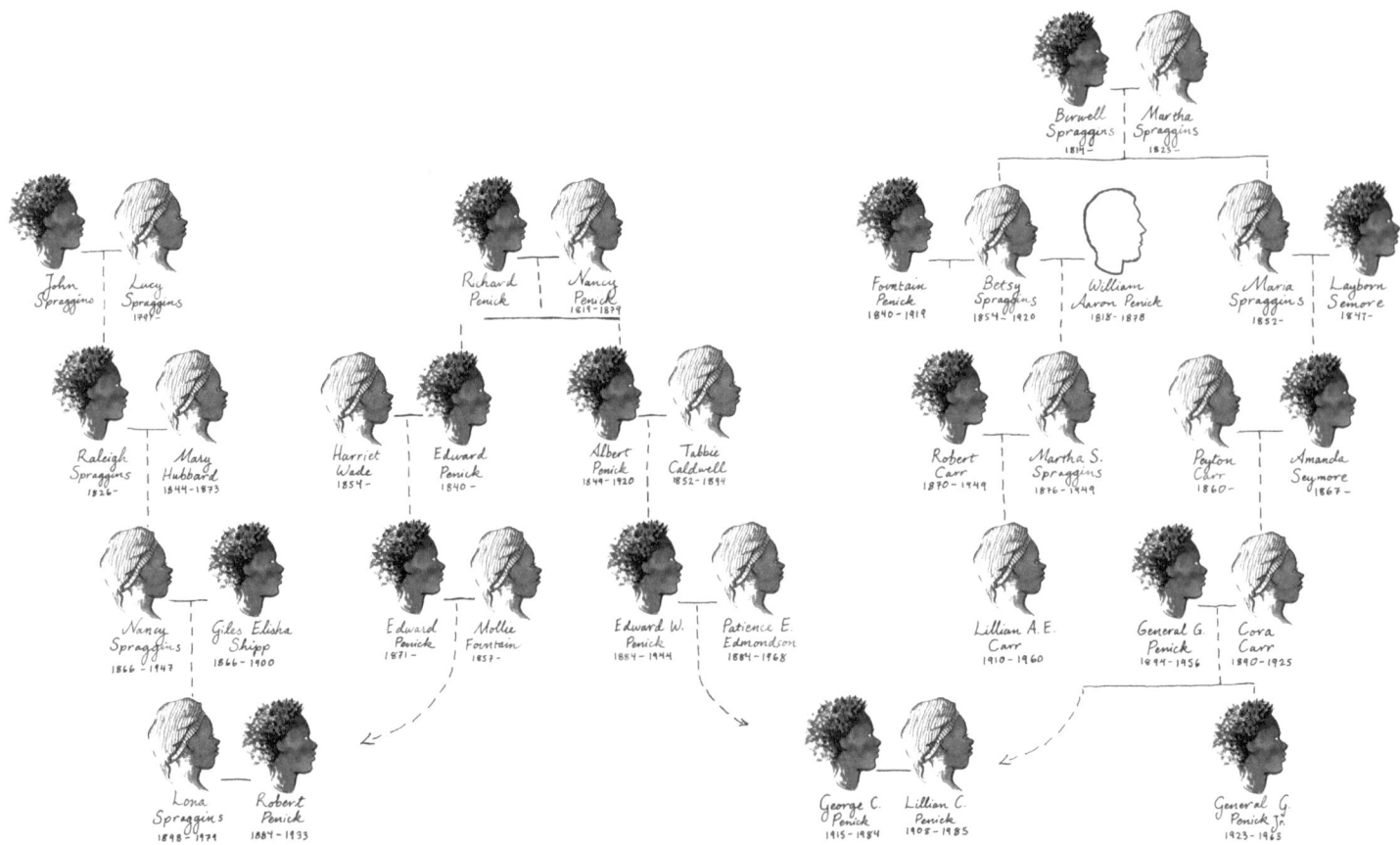

Burwell Spraggins 1814– · Martha Spraggins 1825–

John Spraggins · Lucy Spraggins 1748– · Richard Penick · Nancy Penick 1819–1879 · Fountain Penick 1840–1919 · Betsy Spraggins 1854–1920 · William Aaron Penick 1818–1878 · Maria Spraggins 1852– · Layborn Semore 1847–

Raleigh Spraggins 1826– · Mary Hubbard 1844–1873 · Harriet Wade 1854– · Edward Penick 1840– · Albert Penick 1849–1920 · Tabbie Caldwell 1852–1894 · Robert Carr 1870–1949 · Martha S. Spraggins 1876–1949 · Peyton Carr 1860– · Amanda Seymore 1867–

Nancy Spraggins 1866–1947 · Giles Elisha Shipp 1866–1900 · Edward Penick 1871– · Mollie Fountain 1857– · Edward W. Penick 1884–1944 · Patience E. Edmondson 1884–1968 · Lillian A.E. Carr 1910–1960 · General G. Penick 1894–1956 · Cora Carr 1890–1925

Lona Spraggins 1898–1979 · Robert Penick 1884–1933 · George C. Penick 1915–1984 · Lillian C. Penick 1905–1985 · General G. Penick Jr. 1923–1965

Though I can't be sure that the Rally (Raleigh), Burwell and Martha mentioned in the chancery case are in fact my ancestors, I know there are two African-American Spraggins branches from other ancestral records. I have a hunch that they were related or on the same plantation. Eventually, after several generations and marriages, the Penick and Spraggins lines merged. At the top of this tree, we can find John, Lucy, Martha, and Burwell Spraggins. John and Lucy's great granddaughter Lona Spraggins, married Robert Penick. Martha and Burwell Spraggins had two daughters, Betsy and Maria. Betsy partnered with William Aaron Penick, a white enslaver, and Maria's granddaughter, Cora Carr, married General Grant Penick. The ancestors of General Grant Penick and Robert Penick are, respectively, brothers Albert and Edward Penick.

This is an interwoven and complicated tree, but we can be sure of its veracity because AncestryDNA proves that the descendants of these families are related. In one way or another, these individuals are the descendants of either Raleigh or Martha and Burwell Spraggins *and* Fountain, Albert, or Edward Penick.

Carolyn Hutchinson Brown's *The Sprag(g)ins Family of Virginia* does a thorough job of tracking the Spraggins in Virginia and beyond. The last pages of the book list members of the Spraggins family that Brown had found but couldn't connect to the tree. One of these people is Raleigh J. Spraggins, born in February 1865 and married to Martha Spraggins. At the time of the book's printing in 2003, it would have been difficult for Brown to know that Raleigh and Martha Spraggins were enslaved people who were possibly related to each other and enslaved by their ancestors.

ETYMOLOGY OF "HAIRSTON"

Scottish: habitational name from a place called HARESTONE or HARESTANE.

HAIRSTON PLANTATION STATISTICS

Butter 1000 lbs

96 Sheep

Wheat 400 bushels

Oats 1080 bushels

Potatoes 300 bushels

Honey 26 lbs

Wool 350 lbs

22 Cows

160 Swine

Peas/beans 5 bushels

Sweet Potatoes 55 bushels

Corn 2500 bushels

Flax 10 lbs

Tobacco 7000 lbs

IMPROVED LAND 885 ACRES

UNIMPROVED LAND 7000 ACRES

As mentioned above, Lacy Garlington Smith, Jr's ancestral surnames weren't traceable, except for Hairston. Searching for this name wasn't easy because there were several spelling variations that didn't immediately indicate they were the same family, such as Hurston, Harston, Huston, and Horton. Mat and Kitty (Lacy's great-great grandparents) were the first line I researched, and they have a special place in my heart. Though Mat and Kitty and their thirteen children were born into slavery, they were fortunately freed before they left this earth.

According to census records, Lacy Garlington Smith, Sr's mother, Mary Lena Hairston Smith, was born in Virginia. This was surprising, because I thought all of Lacy Garlington Smith, Jr's family came from North Carolina. I came across birth certificates for Mary Lena's thirteen children. One woman, Charlotte Hairston, is listed as the midwife in almost all of them. I inferred this was Mary Lena's mother, which led me to the 1880 census. At the time of this census, completed fifteen years after the abolition of slavery, Mary Lena was living in Pittsylvania County, VA, with her mother, Charlotte, and father, Joseph.

Surname Tree
HAIRSTON

Mat Hairston
1804 - ?

Kitty Hairston
1819 - ?

Joseph Hairston
1854 - ?

Mary Lena
Hairston
1877 - 1952

Lacy Garlington
Smith Sr.
1895 - 1961

Lacy Garlington
Smith Jr.
1923 - 1983

I knew I needed to find vital records for Charlotte and Joseph because this would allow me to go back one more generation and find their parents. I was able to find their 1875 marriage certificate, and on that beauty of a document, I saw that Joseph's parents were Mat and Kitty from Henry County, VA. Next, I found Mat and Kitty's Cohabitation Register, which listed when they were married, the names and ages of their children, and their last owner, Marshall Hairston.

Finding your ancestors' enslavers is complicated, but in this case, the Hairston enslavers left records I felt conflicted about. I was thankful to have access to these records to learn more about my family, but I also recognized the reasons for writing down this information. The Hairstons were prodigious consolidators of wealth, and their desire to keep it in the family has resulted in nearly 15,000 preserved and cataloged items at the Wilson Library at the University of North Carolina Chapel Hill. These records include correspondence, wills, pardons, ledgers, and other documents that vividly depict the Hairston family, their properties, and the enslaved.

Courtesy of Library of Virginia

Courtesy of Library of Virginia

The Hairston properties extended from Virginia to Mississippi, and they were rumored to have been one of the larger slaveholding families. The Hairstons even piqued the interest of author Henry Weincek, who wrote *The Hairstons: An American Family in Black and White*. His account of the Hairstons brings together disparate threads of the family and is a roadmap to help other genealogists make sense of the breadth of the Hairston estate.

After 1880, Mat and Kitty were lost to history. However, sometime between 1880 and 1900, Joseph Hairston moved to Robeson County, NC (daggone missing 1890 census!). He and Charlotte raised Mary Lena until she married James Smith in 1894. Curiously, the 1920 census shows that Joseph and Charlotte adopted a daughter, Duore Ann McMillian. The records later show two children, Bertie and Lizzie, residing with Mary Lena Smith during the 1930 census. I didn't think anything about it at first, but later, via Bertie's death certificate and AncestryDNA, I was able to link the descendants of Bertie and Lizzie to the Hairston tree. Joseph Hairston had three children with Duore Ann. The family seemingly accepted those children because they remained within the Hairston household for over twenty years, as evidenced by census records.

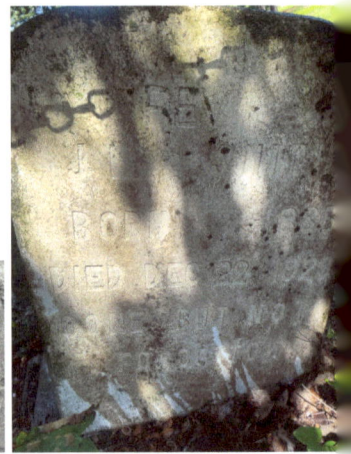

Another part of genealogy research comes from oral histories. Mildred Smith Alexander, a descendant of Claude Douglas Smith, was essential to recreating our family history. Most of my early findings were from her recollections and on-the-ground knowledge of Robeson County, NC. Mildred knew that James Smith was a Reverend, that he preached at St. John Baptist Church, and that he laid the cornerstone at another church. But despite this oral history and my research, we couldn't determine Rev. James Smith's year of death and go back a generation on the Smith side. On a hot and muggy August day with Mildred, some newly discovered cousins, Sandra Oliver, and I found Rev. James Smith's grave in the St. John Baptist Church cemetery. I can't describe the jubilation I found seeing his gravestone. It made the whole journey absolute and final for me. I had been searching for seven months, and here he was right in front of me. It was a wonderful experience of discovering my link to the Smith family's patriarch.

Another piece of history was this picture shared by Marie Elizabeth Smith Chasten's great-granddaughter and the youngest of Rev. James and Mary Lena Smith's children. The picture was of her grandfather, but she never indicated if it was Charles Smith or Joseph Hairston. This is one of the oldest surviving pictures of our ancestors.

ETYMOLOGY OF "SMITH"

English and Scottish: occupational name denoting a worker in metal, especially iron, such as a blacksmith or farrier from Middle English SMITH (Old English SMITH probably a derivative of SMITAN, or "to strike a hammer"

Surname Tree
SMITH

Charles K. Smith
1850 - 1910

James Smith
1875 - 1929

Lacy Garlington Smith Sr.
1895 - 1961

Lacy Garlington Smith Jr.
1923 - 1983

According to the 2010 census, "Smith" is the most frequent surname in the United States. For genealogists, this translates to a research nightmare. Despite the prevalence of "Smith," not all Smiths are related, and untangling those trees can be difficult, as it has proven to be with our Smith ancestors.

James Smith's father's middle initial is "K", and James Smith named his son Donner Kermit Smith. This could be just a coincidence, or perhaps the grandchild was named after the grandfather.

We know James Smith's father is definitively Charles K. Smith because he is listed on his death and marriage certificates as well as Ellen's (James' sister) marriage certificate. However, I've been unable to go further than Charles K. Smith due to the frequency of his surname.

AncestryDNA may help; if Charles K. Smith had siblings and those siblings' descendants submitted their DNA to Ancestry.com, it would be possible to connect them to the descendants of Charles K. Smith. AncestryDNA® ThruLines® analyzes your tree to see if you share DNA with other members' trees. Researchers must be careful with this feature, because incorrect information in either tree will produce flawed results. However, gleaning this information from other trees can help researchers bulk up their own tree.

Ancestry.com indicated, based on other member trees, that Charles K. Smith's parents could be Henry Smith and Rebecca Graham Smith. From historical records, I saw that Rebecca had ten children, though only eight were still living by the 1910 census. One of these children could have been Charles K. Smith, because *his* wife Ellen is listed as a widow in the 1910 census. However, this doesn't definitively prove that Rebecca was his mother.

Tracking a child through census records, especially a male, is not necessarily difficult. Census records list the head of the household and how everyone is related to the head. Children usually leave the household when they get married. The marriage certificate lists the parents' names, whether the parents are living, and place of residence, further confirming this is the same individual from the earlier census. A researcher would then continue to trace the child through their census records and vital records and those of their children, who themselves will marry and have children.

Charles K. Smith isn't present on any censuses with his family because, by the 1870 census, he was presumably old enough to start his household. Thus far, I haven't found a marriage or death certificate linking him to Henry and Rebecca Smith. This means I can take one of two approaches: either assume Henry and Rebecca Smith are his parents or use DNA evidence to make connections.

I won't assume Henry and Rebecca are Charles's parents because Smith is a very frequent surname, and there isn't any certainty that they are related. For the Smith surname, DNA and patience are my best options. More DNA results will continue to be added to the Ancestry.com DNA database, and a descendant of a sibling of Charles may eventually connect to the tree. For now, I have to be careful not to do too much research on this section of the tree because it's predicated on shaky historical ground.

Recreating our ancestors' lives is nearly impossible because we don't have their voices. We can imagine their experiences through newspapers, oral histories, first-hand accounts, and the extant documentation left by their enslavers. Of the surnames I've mentioned, the Hairstons have the most extensive collection of antebellum materials. Although the enslaved aren't always mentioned, they are present in the details. Ann Hairston, the wife of Marshall Hairston, kept a plantation ledger detailing agriculture yield, general store purchases, and recipes. She inadvertently created a genealogical trail, because she mentions the activities and familial relationships of the enslaved people. The Hairston records don't encompass all enslaved experiences, but they do connect us to our history. (Not everyone mentioned is related to our family.) This ledger is a gem among historical records, because of the 30,000 documents I've examined, I've yet to find a more complete history of an antebellum plantation.

The white Hairston family was small, around five people, and the plantation's enslaved fluctuated between 80 and 175 people. The enslaved provided labor for the plantation's operations and created wealth for the Hairston estate. Everything the plantation required, from clothes to wines to meat products, was manufactured by the enslaved. Ann Hairston purchased other items, like buttons, sugar, apples, or silk, from her local general store. The image below is of a letter sheet that Ann could have used, showing she was savvy at finding good prices for her products and purchases. Tax records show that Ann ran the plantation without the assistance of her husband because he's listed as being in Mississippi, probably at their Cooleemee Plantation.

Account book, 1831-1869, in the Hairston and Wilson Family Papers #3149, Southern Historical Collection, Wilson Library, University of North Carolina at Chapel Hill

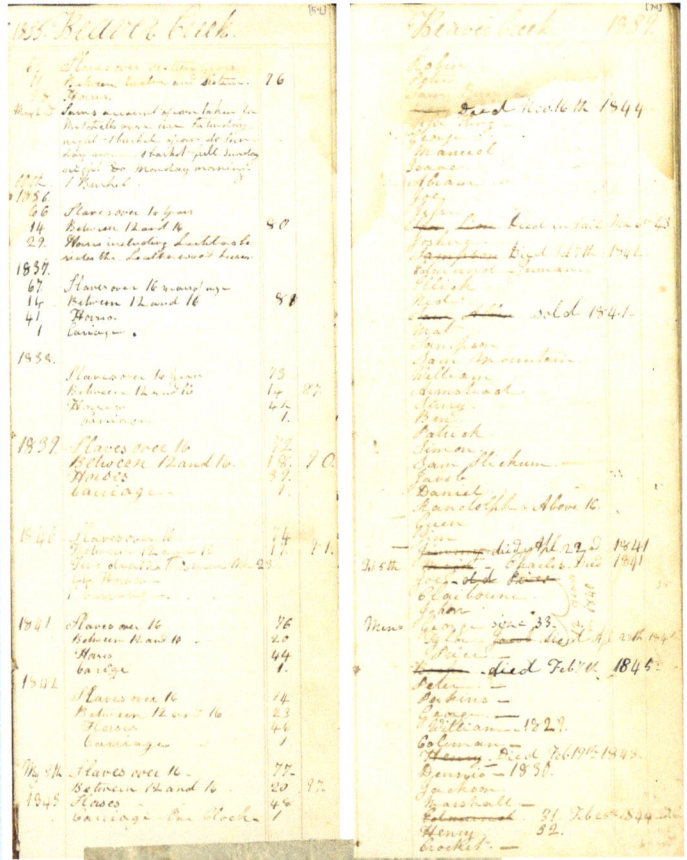

Account book, 1831-1869, in the Hairston and Wilson Family Papers #3149, Southern Historical Collection, Wilson Library, University of North Carolina at Chapel Hill

Clark-Spragins Family Papers (#4440), East Carolina Manuscript Collection, J.Y. Joyner Library, East Carolina University, Greenville, North Carolina, USA

The Hairston's Beaver Creek Plantation occupied over 7,000 acres (885 acres were improved) near Little Beaver Creek. The main house still stands in Henry County, VA, after being rebuilt after an 1839 fire. It is plausible that our ancestors had a hand in rebuilding it because Marshall Hairston would have had free labor to reconstruct his family home. Similarly, this is how Thomas Jefferson built Monticello in neighboring Albemarle County.

The Henry County Table of Tracts of Land for 1863 contains multiple entries for Marshall Hairston. These plots of land total over 7,000 acres but are listed separately due to the survey plats that were recorded over time. As the Hairston clan acquired more land, the ownership changed via a deed, so the land wouldn't be consolidated to a large land mass. I'm sure the Hairston family had a repository of survey plats in their possession so they could keep track of their empire. (This survey plat shows just one 324-acre Beaver Creek section for George Hairston, Marshall Hairston's father.)

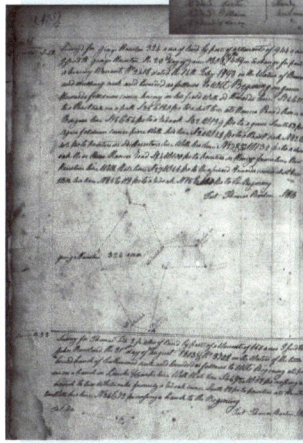

The plantation's size was essential to sustain the horses, sheep, cows, oxen, and tobacco. Growing tobacco strips the land of its nutrients, requiring workers to continually clear new land to keep growing this crop. From Ann Hairston's ledger and federal agriculture schedules, we get a sense of the different areas of plantation production. She tracked potatoes, snaps, onions, horseradish, peppers, onions, yams, honey, and feathers. It is not an exhaustive list, but it shows how the plantation navigated the needs of the fields, animals, and their byproducts. Her ledger shows a yearly rhythm to the plantation operation: agriculture happened between the first and last frost of the year, the first of June was for shearing sheep, fall time was for slaughtering cows and making candles, and the plantation killed hogs in the winter.

One year's sweet potato yield was 55 bushels (one bushel is 50 lbs). One acre could produce 300-350 bushels per year which tells us the sweet potato plot wasn't very large.

Account book, 1831-1869, in the Hairston and Wilson Family Papers #349, Southern Historical Collection, Wilson Library, University of North Carolina at Chapel Hill

Account book, 1831-1869, in the Hairston and Wilson Family Papers #349, Southern Historical Collection, Wilson Library, University of North Carolina at Chapel Hill

Hogs supplied meat for the family, and to avoid spoilage pre-refrigeration, the slaughtered hogs were divided into sections, salted, and smoked with aromatic wood. A 250-pound hog could yield 144 lbs of lard, bacon, chops, chitterlings, hams, ribs, and sausages. Ann Hairston's records show weeks of hog-killing which resulted in her sending large quantities of bacon and lard to neighbors, thanks to the over 160 hogs on the plantation.

Work was constant, because each task was part of a larger process on the plantation ecosystem. Cow's milk was made into butter and sweet cream. Honey and beeswax were harvested as sweeteners and used for home remedies. Flax fields and sheep's wool became thread, yarn, clothing, and household textiles. When not planting and harvesting, the fields needed to be prepared for the next growing cycle. To meet the plantation's demands, the enslaved probably worked from sunup to sundown six days a week. Children were not exempt from plantation labor, either. Those old enough contributed by weeding, carrying water, and watching cattle, and in the tobacco fields, they killed bugs to prevent them from eating the crops.

Ann Hairston traded a pound of bacon for a chicken with one of her enslaved people.
Account book, 1831-1869, in the Hairston and Wilson Family Papers #3149, Southern Historical Collection, Wilson Library, University of North Carolina at Chapel Hill

Account book, 1831-1869, in the Hairston and Wilson Family Papers #3149, Southern Historical Collection, Wilson Library, University of North Carolina at Chapel Hill

Unidentified man standing outside a dilapidated cabin, circa 1910s (The cabin is identified as "Servants house Indian River place."), in the Hairston and Wilson Family Papers #3149, Southern Historical Collection, Wilson Library, University of North Carolina at Chapel Hill

Account book, 1831-1869, in the Hairston and Wilson Family Papers #3149, Southern Historical Collection, Wilson Library, University of North Carolina at Chapel Hill

Ann Hairston's ledger details the yields from the fields, the productivity of her enslaved seamstresses, and, for genealogists, mentions of their ancestors. For example, Ned was a trusted enslaved person who traveled unaccompanied as far as North Carolina to deliver flour and pick up lime and ran other errands for the Hairston family. Other enslaved people include Esther, Grace, Leah, Winny, and Julia, who spun thread and yarn, dyed fabrics, and made clothes for the entire plantation using the yields from the flax fields and sheep herds. These skills weren't insignificant because other formerly enslaved seamstresses achieved great success, and one, Elizabeth Keckley, was even the seamstress to First Lady Mary Todd Lincoln, President Abraham Lincoln's wife. Unbelievably, a post-antebellum letter written by one of Ann Hairston's daughters captures her surprise when Grace chooses not to work for the Hairston family. Ann Hairston's daughter obtusely writes, "I reckon that she thinks she made us rich." The daughter is unable to understand why the enslaved chose freedom over serving the Hairston family.

Account book, 1831-1869, in the Hairston and Wilson Family Papers #3149, Southern Historical Collection, Wilson Library, University of North Carolina at Chapel Hill

Series 1, Correspondence 1863-1865, Folder 10 in the Hairston and Wilson Family Papers #3149, Southern Historical Collection, Wilson Library, University of North Carolina at Chapel Hill

Mat and Kit first appear on page seven of Ann's ledger, along with a mention of their five children. Throughout the pages of the ledger, Mat and Kit's family grows to include grandchildren through their daughter, Independence. They are issued blankets, jackets, pantaloons, shimmies, shoes, and summer and winter clothes. Their mention year after year tells us they were still alive and together as a family, even if enslaved.

Account book, 1831–1869, in the Hairston and Wilson Family Papers #3149, Southern Historical Collection, Wilson Library, University of North Carolina at Chapel Hill

Account book, 1831–1869, in the Hairston and Wilson Family Papers #3149, Southern Historical Collection, Wilson Library, University of North Carolina at Chapel Hill

One aspect of the plantation machine missing from Ann Hairston's ledger is any mention of the tobacco fields. An overseer would most likely have managed this responsibility. She purchased small quantities of tobacco but neglected to write about the tobacco farmed on the plantation. This oversight is covered by the federal agriculture schedule that lists the yields for the Hairston estate. The records show the Hairston estate exceeded the yields of their neighbors and, therefore, required more labor.

Tobacco plots were small, usually just a few acres. They were lucrative but labor-intensive. An acre could produce 500–1,200 lbs of tobacco a year. When not tending to the tobacco, the enslaved worked on other plantation tasks. The Hairston agriculture schedule lists wheat and corn as crops, and these could have been part of a crop rotation protocol to replenish the soil after a season of growing tobacco. The profitable tobacco crop was carefully monitored starting with the preparation of the soil. After burning the fields to kill grass and weeds, tobacco seeds were planted and bushes strategically placed on top to protect from frost while allowing sunlight to filter through. The tobacco plants were coddled with water from neighboring sources, and workers removed weeds and monitored against the tobacco flea beetle and the green horn-worm. Ann Hairston's ledger shows that guinea fowls and turkeys were present on the plantation and they could have been let loose in the fields to tamp down the pests. These birds had a trifecta purpose of pest control, meat and feathers.

This description of the tobacco growing process is quite short. I'd encourage you study it more to better understand our enslaved ancestors' experiences.

Once the tobacco was ripe, workers would cut it, leave it in the field to wilt, and then cure it by air, fire, or flue. The tobacco leaves were removed from their stalks and then packed into hogshead barrels, which could hold about 1,400 lbs of tobacco. The Hairston plantation produced 7,000 lbs of tobacco in one year. With 885 acres of improved land, there were only five other farms (out of 696) that had more improved land in Henry County, VA.

The breadth of the plantation and its operations illustrates the workload of our enslaved ancestors. Most days, from sunrise to sunset, the enslaved completed exhausting work. This work continued for *nearly every day* of their enslavement. If fields needed to be watered, workers carried buckets from the nearest water source. Tilling and weeding were manual tasks that required workers to bend over, because the modern conveniences of tractors, irrigation systems, harvesters, and hale balers didn't exist.

It is no wonder that our ancestors, like Grace, left the plantation to find their own path after the Civil War. Some letters show Ann Hairston complaining that she couldn't find any workers. She asks her daughter to relay to her husband Marshall (who was in Mississippi) to "try for some first-rate white ones and bring them on with you." These letters, which reveal the plantation owners' innermost thoughts, show their low regard for African Americans. In the letters I've read, there seems to be no self-awareness or self-reflection about why they, the white Hairstons, struggled to hire people or convince their former enslaved to stay. We can infer that our enslaved ancestors didn't like the Hairstons or were treated poorly, but I'm inclined to believe that after a lifetime of free labor, they would labor no more for the Hairston family.

Conclusion

Our ancestors were freed from slavery but entered Reconstruction under a new set of rules that placed them in a different type of bondage. Sharecropping, segregation, factory work, and the erosion of civil rights were the remnants of the antebellum period and the white majority's attempt to maintain control and superiority over African Americans. Despite these entrenched biases, we have since earned the right to own property, marry, vote, and receive an education. I'd like to believe that our successes have exceeded what our ancestors could have hoped for, but these triumphs are bittersweet as we still struggle with white America's entrenchment in the upper echelons of society. White America has had a 400-year head start in creating generational wealth that has come at the expense of African Americans' freedom. They continue their subjugation by reversing affirmative action and squashing any outright or perceived attempts by Black Americans to achieve equality and right a 400-year wrong.

The title of this book, *My Name is Not My Own*, acknowledges that my family name has been erased from history. Throughout this research, I've been struck by the number of people who share my family's surnames and how they are all directly linked to white American enslavers. As I navigate America and see street names, neighborhoods, businesses, and politicians with the same name as my ancestral enslavers, I have complex feelings about how the genesis of their wealth was the suffering and disenfranchisement of my ancestors.

*I don't know how this story will end or from whose perspective it will be told, but this story is **our story**. It is our duty and birthright to remember where we came from and never forget that we have earned and deserve a place in American society.*

Bibliography

"African People & the Emerging Atlantic World." Slavery & the Making of the Atlantic World - Chapter I, Section I, National Museum of African American History & Culture, www.searchablemuseum.com/african-people-and-the-emerging-atlantic-world#section-start.

"Europe & the Emerging Global Economy." Slavery & the Making of the Atlantic World - Chapter I, Section III, National Museum of African American History & Culture, https://www.searchablemuseum.com/europe-and-the-emerging-global-economy#section-start.

Hanks, Patrick, et al. Dictionary of American Family Names. Vol. 2, Oxford University Press, 2022.

Hill, H. Edgar. "Descendants of John Flood of Buckingham Co., Virginia." Feb. 2014.

"The Human Cost." Slavery & the Making of the Atlantic World - Chapter IV, Section IV, National Museum of African American History & Culture, https://www.searchablemuseum.com/change-the-human-cost.

Goring, Darlene, "The History of Slave Marriage in the United States" (2006). Journal Articles. 262. https://digitalcommons.law.lsu.edu/faculty_scholarship/262.

OKLAHOMA DEPT. OF AGRICULTURE, FOOD, & FORESTRY. "How Much Meat?"

Robert, Joseph C. The Tobacco Kingdom: Plantation, Market, and Factory in Virginia and North Carolina, 1800-1860. P. Smith, 1965.

"To Grow." Slavery & the Making of a New Nation - Chapter IV, Section VI, National Museum of African American History & Culture, https://www.searchablemuseum.com/to-grow#section-start.

APPENDIX

The Depositions of Giles Shipp taken at Catawba on the 2ᵈ Aug. 1896 by consent of parties by counsel to be read as evidence on behalf of defendants in the Chancery suit of Coates v. Shipp &c. pending in the Circuit Court of Halifax County.

The deponent being first duly sworn deposeth and saith as follows:

1ˢᵗ Question by counsel for defendants.

How old are you?

Answer: I am about thirty two years old.

By same: Were you acquainted with Joseph Shipp and how long did you know him?

Answer: I was born and raised at his house, and lived with him always.

By same: Were you on terms of intimacy with him?

Answer: Yes sir.

By same: What family had he?

Answer: He had no family except his colored people, who were my mother and her children.

By same: Did he talk freely with you or not about his matters?

Answer: Yes sir, as far as any one asked him.

By same: Were you living with him the year that he died, and at the time of his death?

Answer: I was.

By same: What disease did he die of?

Answer: Small Pox.

By same: Did you have the disease also, and if so, was it before or after Joe Shipp had it?

Answer: I had it before he had it.

By same: Who nursed Joe Shipp when he had the

"small boy."

Answer: Joel Brown and myself.

By same: Do you know whether Joe Shipp made a will or not?

Answer: I do not.

By same: Did you ever hear him say whether he had a will or not?

Answer: I heard him say that he did not have a will.

By same: When did you hear him say that he had no will?

Answer: I heard him say it a few days before he died.

By same: Was any other person present besides yourself when he said so?

Answer: Mr. Joel Brown, my wife and myself were present. Mr. Shipp was talking with Mr. Brown.

By same: How did he happen to say that he had no will?

Answer: Mr. Brown asked him if he had a will and he said he had not made any.

By same: What became of Joe Shipp's effects after he died?

Answer: They were sold at the sale.

By same: What became of his papers?

Answer: Mr. Calloway had them. I don't know what became of them.

By same: How did Mr. Calloway get them?

Answer: Mr. Calloway told Mr. Brown and myself after Joe Shipp's death to go into the house and bring him all of the papers of Joseph Shipp

We went into the house and brought all the papers
we could find anywhere and gave them to W. Calloway
who looked through them to his satisfaction. I think we
made as many as three trips for the papers.

By same: Did he find a will of Joseph Shipp among
the papers or elsewhere?

Answer: He said that he could find no will.

By same: Was the side board sold?

Answer: Yes.

By same: Was it kept locked by Joseph Shipp in
his lifetime?

Answer: Yes, I think it was.

By same: Was the house shut up or not after
Joe Shipp's death?

Answer: It was locked up by W. Brown, who
kept the key.

By same: When did Joe Shipp last visit Lynchburg?

Answer: I think it was in June or July of the year
he died.

By same: Did you do any ploughing after you
had the small pox before Joe Shipp died?

Answer: I did not.

By same: Did you see Emily Martin at Joe

Shipp's a few days before he was taken sick,
and after you had the Small Pox?

Answer: I did not.

By same: Could your sister Lucy Shipp read
writing in the lifetime of Joseph Shipp while
he lived there with you all?

Answer: She could not.

By same: Did Mack Jackson take his meals
in Joe Shipp's house while he was detained
at Joe Shipp's, or while he worked there?

Answer: If he did so, I never saw him.

By same: Where did he take his meals?

Answer: He took them in an out house called
the Kitchen.

By same: When did Mack Jackson work at
Joe Shipp's? or did he work there at all?

Answer: He was caught there and was not
allowed to leave, he was never employed to
work at Joe Shipp's, and if he did any work, it
was only what he chose to do while he was
detained on the premises.

By same: Were the premises of Joe Shipp guarded
was to keep people away, and when was the
guard put there?

Answer: A guard was put there, and I think it
was from the time of his death, though I don't
recollect about that.

By same: Did you ever hear Mack Jackson
or Lucy Shipp say in the lifetime of Joseph
Shipp that he had a will?

Ans: I never heard Mack say anything about it.

I heard Lucy say that she believed he had a will.

By same: Did she say to whom she believed he had given his property?

Answer: She said she believed he had willed his property to ~~his~~ us, his coloured people.

By same: Did she say that she had seen his will, or only believed that he had a will?

Answer: She did not say that she had seen it— only that she believed he had a will.

By same: Was Joe Shipp more intimate with Mack Jackson or you?

Answer: Greatly more intimate with me.

By same: Have you any recollection of Mack Jackson being at Joe Shipp's barn with Joe Shipp when firing tobacco?

Answer: None in the world.

By same: Who generally fired his tobacco?

Answer: Tom Jackson, I reckon, as Tom made it.

By same: Did Joe Shipp do it?

Answer: He had no tobacco the year he died, nor made any but willed out his land. He did not fire any tobacco.

X Exam. 1st question by Plffs Councel.

What kin was Tom Jackson to Mack Jackson?

Ans. I think they were Cousins.

By Same. Can you pretend to say that you know that Mack Jackson never worked on Joe Shipps

premises during the year in which he died or that
he never fired or helped fire a barn of Tob. for
him or Tom Jackson?

Ans. I don't know, I can't say of my own knowledge that he didn't. He staid there some time
but I don't know what he did.

By Same. Were you married at the time of Jos Shipps
death?

Ans. Yes Sir.

By Same. Where did you & your wife & family stay?

Ans. We lived in a house about three quarters
of a mile from his house until he was
taken with the Small pox & then we came
& staid in the house with him until he died.

By Same. How do you know that Mack Jackson
never took his meals in Joe Shipps house?

Ans. I know that he never did from the time
I went there when he was taken with the Small
pox, He might have done so before I went
there. I don't know about that.

By Same. Where did Lucy Shipp stay?

Ans. She staid in the house with him.

By Same. Could she read & spell any?

Ans. I think she could read a little when he
died.

By Same. When did he die?

Ans. It was in the fall I think, I can't recollect the
month or year.

By Same. How long had You been up & well of the Small pox before Joe Shipp was taken sick?

Answ. I don't recollect how long it was, but I was so I could get about right well.

By Same. Emily Martin has stated that she was at Joe Shipp's about two weeks before he was taken sick. Do you mean to say that she is mistaken & that she was not there at that time?

Answ. No Sir — She might have been there, but I never saw her.

By Same. How long were you sick with the Small pox

Answ. Three weeks

By Same. Can you undertake to say that You know all that happened on Joe Shipp's premise & who came there & what he did & where he went during the 3 weeks of yr sickness?

Answ. No Sir — I know nothing about what was done &c while I was sick away from there.

By Same. Did you ever ask Joel Brown to go & see Joe:
    Shipp about making his will?

Ansr. No Sir.

By Same. Did not Joe Shipp say in your presence in
    talking about his will, that he had his matters
    all fixed?

Ansr. No Sir. he didnt say so

By Same. Have you never stated that he did say so?

Ansr. I dont know particular whether I ever did or
    not.

By Same. Did he say he wanted to make a will or
    wd. or intended to write one himself?

Ansr. He said to Mr Brown, he didnt have no will, but
    wd. be so he coved attend to his own business in
    a few days but said nothing about making
    a will.

                    5366

By Same. Do you recollect taking any papers out of
    his Sideboard after his death?

    Ansr. Mr Brown took them out himself

By Same: Did you ever see her use them?

Answer: I never did.

By Same: Do you know that became of the papers of Joe Shift after his death?

Answer: I was present when Mr. Calloway the administrator of Joseph Shift, sent Mr. Brown and Giles Shift to get the papers. He told them to go into the house and examine everywhere and bring him every paper. They went into the house and brought out papers as many as three times, I know, if not oftener.

By Same: Were the papers examined by Mr. Calloway as brought to him by Mr. Brown and Giles Shift?

Answer: They were.

By Same: Did Calloway or any one else find any will of Joe Shift?

Answer: He was asked several times by bystanders if there was any will, and he said there was none.

By Same: Were the people, except Mr. Brown and Giles Shift, afraid to go into the house?

Answer: I suppose so. None of us went within a hundred yards of the house.

By Same: ~~Absolutely~~

X Examd. Are you on friendly terms with your Sister?

Ans. Yes Sir, as far as I know.

By same. Are you in the habit of visiting her?

Ans. I haven't been there for 10 or 12 months but have been there since the War.

By same. Do you know that she never uses spectacles?

Ans. I never saw her use them &

never heard of it until today.

By Same. Did you ever see her reading or trying to read?

Ansr. Many a time. I went to a school with her.

By Same. You never saw her read then since she left school?

Ansr. Yes I have.

By Same. When?

Ansr. I couldn't tell you when. Many years ago. I have seen very little of her for 20 years.

By Same. How far do you live from your Sister?

Ansr. About a mile.

By Same. Do you mean to say that you are on entirely friendly terms with her & haven't been to see her for 10 or 12 months & the lives but a mile from you?

Ansr. Yes Sir, we are entirely friendly.

By Same. Can you say that you have seen her reading or engaged in anything requiring the use of eye glasses at any time within the last 5 or 6 years?

Ansr. I have seen her within the last twelve months at her house sewing without spectacles.

By Same. How are you interested in the result of this suit.

Ansr. I have ~~got nothing~~ to do with it that I know of.

By Same. Do you not feel a very deep interest in the result of this suit?

Ansr. Why should I? — No I don't feel no deep interest in the result of this suit.

By Same. Have you not stated that you intended to defend this suit & also you were not interested more than a few hundred

By Same. Where did he get the Key from?

Ans. He had the Key.

By Same. Do You Know who bought the Sideboard?

Ans. Joshua Francis has it now. I think Geo Coates bought it at the sale.

Ex: in Chief resumed.

Question by counsel for plaintiff:

Did you ever hear Joe Shipp say what he meant to do with his property after his death?

Answer: I heard him say that he never wanted David Shipp, Geo. Coates, and Nancy Coates nor any of her children to have a ninepence worth of any of his property. I heard him say it on his death bed the morning Mr. Brown was talking with him.

By same: Did you ever hear say the same at any other time?

Answer: I reckon I have heard him say it 500 times.

By same: Is Tom Coates a child of Nancy Coates?

Answer: Yes Sir.

By same: From whom did Joe Shipp get his property?

Answer: His mother gave it to him.

By same: Did Tom Coates ever live with Joe Shipp after the death of Joe Shipp's mother?

Answer: I dont think he did. He lived with them before her death. Joe Shipp and his mother lived together.

By same: You have said that Lucy Shipp could read a little — do you mean that she could read a little of printing or writing?

Answer: I think she could read a little of printing in a spelling book. She could not read such printing as the bible.

Ex: in Chief resumed:

How long did Tom Coates live there and when did he leave?

Answer: He lived there a good while and left a good many years before the war. He left after Joe Shipp's mother died, and she died when I was ten years old. I am now 32.

And further this Deponent saith not.

its Alex E Shipp

The Deposition of George Coates taken at the same time and place and for the same purpose.

The deponent being first duly sworn deposeth and saith as follows:

Question by counsel for defdt.

State whether you ever had any conversation with Mack Jackson in regard to Joe Shipp's having a will — when it was and what he said?

Answer: After Joe Shipp's death — I dont recollect the year, David Shipp and myself were pulling fodder in the fall of the year, and I saw Mack Jackson going through the plantation. I stopped him and asked him what he knew of Uncle Joe Shipp's will. He said he knew nothing about it. I then asked Mack if Uncle Joe ever told him he had a will. He answered that he did not — that Joe Shipp never told him about his will — that he never knew anything about his having a will.

By same: Did any one hear this conversation besides yourself?

Answer: David Shipp heard it.

By same: Did Joe Shipp make any will the year he died?

Answer: He did when he rented out his land, I think to Tom Jackson.

And further Deponent saith not.

his
George L Coates
mark

The Deposition of David Shipp taken at the same time and place and for the same purpose.

The Deponent being first duly

1

The deposition of Lucy Shipp taken in
the Clerk office of the Kentucky court
for the county of Danville on the
18th day of December 1876 to be read
in evidence upon the trial of a suit in
chancery now pending in the
Circuit court of Halifax in which
Thomas Coats is plaintiff and Nancy
Coats & others are defendants

        The deponent being
first duly sworn deposeth & sayeth as follows
Question by plaintiffs counsel Were
you acquainted with Joseph Shipp late
of Halifax County

Answer I was very well acquainted with
him knew him all my life. My
Master belonged to him I have been
there third with him till he died

By same when & when did he die & what
was the matter with him

Answer He died in Halifax county after
~~the~~ his surrender I don't know the
day he died but remember now he died
with the measles pox

By same do you know whether or not
he made a will

Answer yes sir He made a will not
long before he died

By Jury How do you know

Answer He did me do it and it was
I taught me to put it in the little leather
trunk & put it in the old Board

By Jury Who wrote the will

Answer He wrote it himself

By Jury do you know what became
of the will
Answer I do not. It laid in his House
a short time before he died & left the
House wrote as he was taken back
with the made post

This beautiful specimen was left
thoughtlessly unfinished
Copy by me W Pope MP
18 Dec 1846

will—that I must sign, and that this was—
the House when I left.

By Same How do you know it was the—
House when you—left

Answer: I knew it it was—in the
Board in the little Trunk.

By Same "Do you understand what the
will contained if you do repeat the
language as near as you can

Answer: Me my Mother & Sister was to have
a Home as long as we wished & Tom Coats
was to have the delivery. I think the
language was as follows. I give my
property to Thomas Coats, but my Women
& two of their clapps, Lucy & Susan
are to have a home in my land as
long as they wish or as long as they live
This was the substance of the will I
knew.

By Same How do you know that this
was the language & substance of the
will

Answer: Master Jerkeph told me so & he
read it to me so

By Same Do you know whether he was,
really with his Sister & Nancy Coats &
her other children

Answer. I know he was, very unfriendly
with myself & money, & her other children
I have heard him say that they never
should have any of his property. that
he intended to will it all to master Tom
Coats. he raised Tom Coats & was always
very ready with him. master Tom never
had much ado with his mother or any of
her children he never stood with any
of them that I ever heard of. when
I came can't remember master Tom was
living with master's

By whom. Can you read.
Answer. I can read a little. can't read
      writing.
By whom. did you read the will or any
      part of it.
Answer. I did not. because I can't read
      writing.
By whom. were you at home at the time
      the House was burnt
Answer. I was,
By whom. was the will brought out at that
      time
Answer. I do not know they brought out all the
      papers in a basket & burnt them — at some
      of them they brought out a basket of old
      papers & burnt them — I told Giles, who

bringing the things out that she wished —
a little Leather trunk in the Side Board
I was there in the yard but they would
not let me to go in the House. Giles
had had the small pox & they let him
go in to get the things out to Burn —
I don't know whether he brought the
little trunk out or not. Nor do I know
whether the will was then in the trunk
all I know is that it was in that
little leather trunk in the Side Board,
when I left the House. They brought the
Basket of papers out to the Table yard
where Mr Callaway was, for him to
look at them before they burnt them —

My James was Nimmy Coats there the day
the things were moved out of the House
was burnt

Answer She was there

My James do you know what became of that
little leather trunk

Answer I do not. I have never seen it since
I left the House when May Joe was
taken sick with the Small pox — I had
not had the Small pox at the time the
House was burned. but I took it after
Master died & got well of it.

By James. Was any of Nancy Coats children
There when the House was burnt

Answer Yes. Geo. Coats & her son-in-law
William Times & others

By James How did you come to take this Wife was in the little Trunk in the Silk Band.

Answer I was afraid that Miss Nancy or
some of her children would get
hold of it & carry it to Mitchell Coats.
that it was in the little Trunk & I Wished to
carry it to one Mitchell Spickman
a cabinet maker because I knew that
promises had been made for my mother
Myself & my sister & I did not want it
Destroyed. And further this deponent
saith not

                            his
                    Lucy X Shipp
                            mark

The foregoing Deposition was taken
obtained sworn to before me at the
time & place & for the purpose mentioned
in the Caption given under my hand
this the 18th December 1876.

                    W. Riew N.P.

The reading of the within deposition is excepted to because taken without notice to any of the defendants or their counsel. It was not known until to day that it had been taken.

John W. Kiely
Counsel for Defts
July 19 1877

Additional Powell Family Documents

Nelson 1888

REGISTER OF MARRIAGES

[7—296.]

Received July 24, 1880

Page No. 5-8

Supervisor's Dist. No. 3

Enumeration Dist. No. 111

Note A.—The Census Year begins June 1, 1879, and ends May 31, 1880.

Note B.—All persons will be included in the Enumeration who were living on the 1st day of June, 1880. No others will. Children BORN SINCE June 1, 1880, will be OMITTED. Members of Families who have DIED SINCE June 1, 1880, will be INCLUDED.

Note C.—Questions Nos. 13, 14, 22 and 23 are not to be asked in respect to persons under 10 years of age.

196

SCHEDULE 1.—Inhabitants in *Lovingston District* , in the County of *Nelson* , State of *Virginia* enumerated by me on the *25* day of June, 1880.

William J. Bidd

Enumerator.

CERTIFICATE OF DEATH — COMMONWEALTH OF VIRGINIA — 27170

www.ingramcontent.com/pod-product-compliance
Lightning Source LLC
Chambersburg PA
CBHW041549260326
41914CB00016B/1591